Living in Absolute
FREEDOM

Bethany House Books
by Donna Partow

Becoming a Vessel God Can Use
Living in Absolute Freedom
Walking in Total God-Confidence

Living in Absolute
FREEDOM

Donna Partow

BETHANY HOUSE PUBLISHERS
MINNEAPOLIS, MINNESOTA 55438

Published by Bethany House Publishers
A Ministry of Bethany Fellowship International
11400 Hampshire Avenue South
Minneapolis, Minnesota 55438
www.bethanyhouse.com

Printed in the United States of America by
Bethany Press International, Minneapolis, Minnesota 55438

Library of Congress Cataloging-in-Publication Data

Partow, Donna.
    A ten-week journey to living in absolute freedom / by Donna Partow.
      p. cm.
    ISBN 0–7642–2292–9 (pbk.)
    1. Christian women—Religious life.
2. Liberty—Religious aspects—Christianity.
I. Title: Living in absolute freedom. II. Title.
BV4527 .P375   2000
248.8'43—dc21   00–008107
                                            CIP

To my daughter, Taraneh Joy

"They will be called oaks of righteousness,
a planting of the Lord
for the display of his splendor.
They will rebuild the ancient ruins
and restore the places long devastated. . . .
Their descendants will be known among the nations
and their offspring among the peoples.
All who see them will acknowledge
that they are a people the Lord has blessed."

Isaiah 61:3b–4a, 9

DONNA PARTOW is a Christian communicator with a compelling testimony of God's transforming power. From her childhood as "the kid no one was allowed to play with" to her days as a drug dealer and her marriage to a strict Middle Eastern husband, she shares her life journey with disarming honesty and humor.

Donna's uncommon transparency and passion for Christ have been used by God at women's conferences and retreats around the country. She has been a popular guest on more than two hundred radio and TV programs, including *Focus on the Family*.

She is the bestselling author of numerous books including *Becoming a Vessel God Can Use* and *Walking in Total God-Confidence*.

If your church sponsors an annual women's retreat, perhaps they would be interested in learning more about Donna's special weekend program on "Living in Absolute Freedom." For more information, contact:

Donna Partow
P.O. Box 842
Payson, AZ 85541
(520) 472–7368
donnapartow@cybertrails.com

Special Thanks

To my heavenly Father.
You set my spirit free.

To Rachell Sampson,
for being such a servant-hearted helper.
It sounds cliché, but I literally couldn't have done it
without you.

To my editor, Steve Laube,
for fielding all the weird phone calls.

And to the staff at Bethany House,
for giving me the freedom to share the message
God has laid on my heart.

Contents

WEEK ONE: FACE YOUR BONDAGE, PART ONE
   SLAVERY DEFINED

Day One: Introduction 13
Day Two: Slavery Defined. 18
Day Three: On the Outside Looking In 22
Day Four: Escape and Recapture 26
Day Five: The Drift Toward Slavery 30

WEEK TWO: FACE YOUR BONDAGE, PART TWO
   LEGALISM VERSUS LICENSE

Day One: Slaves to Sin 36
Day Two: Legalism Versus License 41
Day Three: Enslaved by Legalism 46
Day Four: Enslaved by License 50
Day Five: Liberty 54

WEEK THREE: FACE YOUR BONDAGE, PART THREE
   SOLD CHEAP

Day One: Sold to Financial Security 60
Day Two: Sold to the Relentless Pursuit of Status 63
Day Three: Sold to the Status Quo. 67
Day Four: Sold Into Slavery 72
Day Five: Enslaved by Another's Choices 77

WEEK FOUR: RECEIVE YOUR DELIVERER

Day One: Our Deliverer Is Coming 82
Day Two: Our Deliverer Has Come 85
Day Three: Who Will Deliver Me? 88
Day Four: God, My Champion 91
Day Five: From the River to the Sea 94

WEEK FIVE: EMBRACE YOUR LIBERTY

Day One: Liberating Your Heart 100
Day Two: Liberating Your Mind, Part One 104
Day Three: Liberating Your Mind, Part Two 107
Day Four: Liberating Your Spirit 111
Day Five: Liberating Your Will 115

WEEK SIX: EMANCIPATE YOUR FELLOW SLAVES, PART ONE

Day One: Quit Messing With My Kids 120
Day Two: The Prison of Expectations 124
Day Three: Stop the Blame Game 129
Day Four: Setting the Captives Free Through Forgiveness 134
Day Five: They're Making Me Sin 137

WEEK SEVEN: EMANCIPATE YOUR FELLOW SLAVES, PART TWO

Day One: The Broken Places, Part One 142
Day Two: The Broken Places, Part Two 146
Day Three: Redeeming the Broken Places 149
Day Four: Her Broken Place 152
Day Five: The Ceremony 156

WEEK EIGHT: DELIGHT YOURSELF IN GOD

Day One: Delight Yourself in God 162
Day Two: Delight in the God Who Rules 166
Day Three: Delight Yourself in God's Word 170
Day Four: Delight in the God Who Is Worthy to Be Praised 175
Day Five: Delight in the God Who Delights in You 178

Contents

WEEK NINE: OVERCOME POCKETS OF RESISTANCE

Day One: Higher Ground...................................... 186
Day Two: Overcoming Doubt............................... 189
Day Three: Overcoming Conflicting Desires 192
Day Four: Overcoming the Fear of Man 197
Day Five: Overcoming the Power of Lies 201

WEEK TEN: MOVE FORWARD IN ABSOLUTE FREEDOM

Day One: Set Free to Live Free.............................. 206
Day Two: Life in the Promised Land 210
Day Three: Freedom Through Remembrance.................. 214
Day Four: To Know What's in Your Heart 218
Day Five: Free to Embrace Both the Price and the Privilege 222

Steps to Freedom... 227
A Note to Leaders 229

WEEK ONE:

Face Your Bondage, Part One
Slavery Defined

This Week's Verse:

It is for freedom that Christ has set us free. Stand firm then
and do not let yourselves be burdened again by
a yoke of slavery.

Galatians 5:1

Day One

Introduction

It is for freedom that Christ has set us free. Stand firm then and do not let yourselves be burdened again by a yoke of slavery.

Galatians 5:1

Prior to the Emancipation Proclamation, slaves who tried to escape on their own, following an uncharted path, were usually recaptured. Then something wonderful happened: slaves who had successfully escaped to the North established the Underground Railroad. They did not become so complacent in their freedom that they forgot what it was to live as slaves. And so they did more than point the way for others. They risked everything to go back and walk again the path to freedom—not for their own sakes but for the sake of their fellow sojourners. When the slaves realized they would be led by those who had escaped, those who knew the route by personal painful experience, it gave them greater confidence to attempt escape themselves.

While I don't claim to be risking *everything*—certainly not my physical life—in charting this spiritual underground railroad, I will risk being vulnerable. I will risk sharing with you my personal painful experiences on the journey to freedom.

If you're going to risk escape, I think you have the right to know who is leading you on the journey. Is it someone who has *read* about ways to escape? Is it someone who has *thought* a lot about ways to escape? Is it someone who has developed *theories* about ways to escape? Is it someone who has sat in an office and *listened* to other people tell about how they escaped?

Or has this person *actually* escaped? Does she know from experience what it is to live in bondage? And has she found a way to live in freedom?

Please, let me assure you: *I know what it is to live in bondage.* And I have traveled the path to freedom. Now, mind you, I've been recaptured a time or two. On the bright side, that means I've also traveled the road a time or two—so I am *very* familiar with the path.

My analogy to the Underground Railroad is not a perfect one, of course, because we are living *after* the Emancipation Proclamation. Christ has set us free. The problem is, many of us continue to live like slaves. The apostle Paul wrote, "It is for freedom that Christ has set us free. Stand firm then and do not let yourselves be burdened again by a yoke of slavery" (Galatians 5:1). Far too many Christians, having been set free, allow themselves to be burdened again by a yoke of slavery. They become enslaved to legalism or license. They become enslaved to other people's opinions of them. They become enslaved to materialism, status, and wrong priorities. Having been set free, our mission is to escape a life of volunteer slavery.

Although you can take this journey alone, I would encourage you to take it with friends. Ideally this study should be completed as part of a weekly Bible study. However, you can gather informally with a small group or with just one friend. Even if you opt to go it alone, you won't be completely alone. You'll have me as your traveling companion and God as your conductor.

When taking a journey of this nature, it helps to know the lay of the land, to have the overall route in mind before you actually begin traveling the road. So, if possible, quickly read through the entire book to get an overview.[1] Then go back and work through the study, one day at a time, carefully answering the questions, memorizing the weekly verses, and studying the review material.

I recently received a hilarious e-mail from a woman who was teaching my previous study, *Walking in Total God-Confidence,* to a group at her church. She said that during the first few weeks of the study she couldn't understand why I asked EVERY DAY, "What key lesson did you glean from today's study?" Here's what she had to say:

> We love the word glean. At first, we would laugh whenever
> we said it (especially me), until we read the definition. Glean—
> to gather little by little, to collect with patient effort. Awesome!

---

[1] I include this suggestion at the urging of many readers of my previous books who say they have found it very beneficial to get an initial overview before completing the study.

Do you mean God wants us to be patient, and he's not going to change us overnight? Anyhow, now we all love the word "glean."[2]

As you work through this study, I'll ask you to apply the gleaning principle: Every day, little by little, patiently gather truths from God's Word. Don't skip any of the questions! (I have ways of checking up on you.) In particular, don't miss your daily gleaning opportunity. I've also given you the daily opportunity of writing out a prayer to God. This is such a wonderful spiritual discipline to develop. At first it may feel awkward; your prayers may be rote. Stick with it. I believe God speaks powerfully through a pen and some blank space. As you grow in "prayer journaling," you may find that you want more room than I've allowed. That's great. Buy a notebook, and if you run out of space on a particular day, finish writing your prayer in the notebook.

It is the earnest prayer of my heart that God will choose to meet with you on the pages of this book, that you will hear *his voice*, not mine. Even so, completing a ten-week Bible study is a serious commitment. It won't be easy. At times you'll want to quit. You'll want to turn back to your former way of life. At least your old taskmasters were familiar, and sometimes familiar bondage seems preferable to unfamiliar freedom. It isn't. So resist the temptation to surrender. Whatever hazards you face, whatever pain you endure, true freedom is worth the sacrifice. Mentally prepare yourself now. Make the commitment. Say it out loud if you need to: *I will finish the journey I've started, no matter what it takes*.

Reflections Along the Journey

1. Have you been set free in Christ? If you have any doubts, please turn to the back of the book and review the Steps to Freedom. If yes, write a brief testimony of how you came to freedom and be ready to share this with your group.

---

[2]E-mail from Nicole Lacroix.

2. Having been set free, are you truly *living free,* or do you feel like you've been "burdened again by a yoke of slavery"? Describe.

3. What do you hope to gain from this study? List some of your goals.

4. Write out a prayer to God, expressing your desire to live in absolute freedom.

5. What key lesson did you glean from today's study?

Freedom Truths:

- We have been set free to live free.
- If we are living in bondage, it is voluntary slavery.

Day Two

Slavery Defined

There is no fear in love. But perfect love drives out fear.
1 John 4:18

I define slavery as "anything that holds you back from being and doing all that God has created you to be and do." Throughout the coming weeks I'll share various things (and even people!) to whom I've been in bondage. Having shared this message with thousands of women, I've discovered that slavery takes different shapes for each of us. I may describe some forms of slavery to which you respond, "Wow! I can't believe you lived in bondage to that! I've never had a problem in that area." My bondage to Oreo cookies may be a case in point! Other manifestations of slavery appear almost universal—like being enslaved to other people's opinions.

Although some of us are, in fact, living in literal bondage, more often the problem exists in our own hearts and minds. Unfortunately mental, spiritual, and emotional bondages are just as real as physical bondages. Put another way, anything that you BELIEVE is holding you back IS holding you back from being and doing all that God has created you to be and to do.

Let me share an illustration that explains what I mean. Several years ago I was caught off guard when . . . the elephants started coming. Every time I turned around, another elephant was marching into my life. Stuffed elephants, elephant earrings, an elephant belt, even an elephant planter. Mind you, I didn't go looking for this stuff; it came looking for me.

Well, I've been a Christian long enough to know that maybe, just maybe, God was trying to get a message through to me. After all, if God could speak through Balaam's donkey (Numbers 22), he could speak through elephants. So I began thinking about it. *OK, Lord, what are you trying to tell me? Go easy on the Oreos, maybe?*

But I knew that a God of love would never send a message like that! Then I heard the story of how elephants are brought into captivity. Have you ever been to a circus and observed a giant elephant with a small rope around its ankle? Did you ever stop to think, *Hey, wait a minute. Physically speaking, there is no way that dinky little rope can hold back that giant elephant!* And did you ever wonder how it happened that a giant elephant can be held in place by something that does not have the power to contain him?

Here's how it works. When trainers begin taming a baby elephant, they place a heavy chain around its ankle and stake the chain into the ground. Day after day, hour after hour, the baby elephant struggles to escape. But his efforts are in vain. He simply cannot break free from the grip of that powerful chain. Eventually he surrenders. He resolves in his mind that there is no possible way he can escape that chain. So he relinquishes forever the struggle to be free.

Then when he has given up trying, his masters replace that giant chain with the dinky little rope. If the elephant ever opened his eyes to the truth, he could break free at any moment. All it would take is one try, but since the elephant doesn't know that, he doesn't take a step in the direction of freedom.

And so it happens that ten, twenty, thirty years later, the giant elephant remains held in bondage by something that really has NO POWER to control him, except the power he chooses to give it. When I first heard this story, a voice cried out within me, *Donna, that's you! You're allowing your life to be controlled by things that no longer have the power to control you, except the power that you—in your own twisted little mind—are choosing to give them.*

Is this true for you as well? The apostle Paul wrote, "It is for freedom that Christ has set us free. Stand firm then and do not let yourselves be burdened again by a yoke of slavery" (Galatians 5:1). When Christ went to the cross, he broke the chains that bind us. He set us free from the power of sin and death. If you have trusted Christ for your salvation, you're no longer in bondage: "For if you tell others with your own mouth that Jesus Christ is your Lord, and believe in your own heart that God has raised him from the dead, you will be saved" (Romans 10:9 TLB).

If you have *not* taken that step of faith, the chains are *real*. You're like that baby elephant who literally cannot escape. You cannot escape the penalty for your sins, nor can you escape the guilt, fear, and shame that haunt those who haven't made things right with their Creator. At the back of this book, you'll find "Steps to Freedom." If you have any doubts about where you stand—free, or in bondage—I would urge you to turn to these steps now. Think and pray about the passages and truths presented. If you are part of a weekly study group, talk to your discussion leader, and make sure you get connected with a solid, Bible-teaching church.

OK, let's assume that's resolved. You have been set free in Christ, and therefore the *chains* have been broken. You've been set free to live free. If you're not *living free*, it's probably because you (or someone else) has tied some dinky little rope around your ankle. Since you haven't taken a close enough look, you're giving that rope far more power than it deserves.

Usually the rope is some type of fear: fear of failure, fear of success, fear of rejection, fear of man. Examine your rope. Name the fear, and remember that perfect love, which is the love we have in Christ, casts out fear. "There is no fear in love. But perfect love drives out fear" (1 John 4:18).

That's exactly what this ten-week journey is designed to help you do. Throughout *Living in Absolute Freedom*, I want you to ponder: *Am I still living like I'm in chains? Lord, show me how. Give me the courage to shake my foot loose and walk away, knowing I've been set free to live in absolute freedom.*

I pray that many who are reading these words will enter into a new sense—a deeper reality—of the freedom we have in Christ.

Reflections Along the Journey

1. Are you in any way like that giant elephant held in bondage by a rope? Describe.

2. Can you think of something you would do right now if you were truly free?

3. What is it that is holding you back? Identify your "rope," your fear. Pray that God's love will cast it out!

4. Write out a prayer thanking God for your freedom.

5. What key lesson did you glean from today's study?

Freedom Truths:

- We have been set free to *live* free.
- Slavery is anything that prevents you from being and doing all God has in mind for you.

Day Three

On the Outside Looking In

Therefore, there is now no condemnation for those who are in Christ Jesus.

Romans 8:1

Although I promise to resist the temptation to transform this book into my autobiography,[3] I want to share with you something of my life in slavery. I think it will help you understand why I feel so passionately about the importance of living in the absolute freedom Christ has called us to.

I was born in a suburb of Philadelphia, the youngest of eight children. My father was a truck driver, and my mom stayed home to raise us kids. Aside from the occasional chaos you'd expect in a family of eight kids, our life was normal. We had our ups and downs, but the ups seemed to have the upper hand. Then came the Vietnam War. Everything changed. We had grown up on WWII stories glamorized by John Wayne movies. My dad was a paratrooper with the legendary 101st Airborne—recently made even more famous in the Academy Award-winning movie *Saving Private Ryan*. So it was natural for my oldest brother, Jimmy, to report to the local recruiting station and enlist in the 101st Airborne.

Unfortunately Vietnam was far from a John Wayne movie. The first week in combat, my seventeen-year-old brother watched all but one of his fellow soldiers get massacred. He rescued his lieutenant, and leaving behind eighty-three mutilated bodies, he walked for miles through enemy-infested jungle to a military hospital, where he do-

---

[3]To those of you who've read my previous books, I realize you are already familiar with these stories, so please bear with me today and tomorrow as I present my testimony for the benefit of those who are just "joining the club." Thanks!

nated blood to save the lieutenant's life, even though my brother had lost blood from his own gunshot wound.

I won't tell the whole tale of his Vietnam adventure, but I will tell you he returned a mere shadow of his former self. Worst of all, he returned addicted to heroin. For reasons I've struggled my whole life to understand, there was fertile soil for drug abuse in my family. Maybe it was just life in the 1960s. I had always suspected imperfect parenting, until I had children of my own and realized my parents did a great job.

Whatever the cause, it wasn't long before four of my family members were addicted to heroin. I cannot begin to describe the hell our family lived through. If you love an alcoholic or a drug addict, you already know. If you don't, no words can help you to understand the magnitude of the bondage.

The police became involved. There were front-page news stories in our small-town paper. Soon everyone knew we were a family in trouble. The people who had put up banners welcoming the hero home now banned their kids from coming to our house. All of a sudden we were the bad-news family and I was the kid in the neighborhood no one was allowed to play with.

I can remember how the kids in my class would torment me relentlessly. They would draw pictures of my family with needles in our arms and write "Drug Addict Family" across the top. I'll never forget one day in particular: the teacher stepped out of the room and all the kids in my class formed a circle around me and taunted, "Drug addict family, drug addict family, drug addict family," until I couldn't stand it anymore and ran home crying.

Very few days in my childhood loom darker than that one. But there was an especially dark night—the memory of which I've struggled to break free from all my life. My next-door neighbor had a birthday party. She invited everyone in the class—except me. I knew the festivities were taking place; occasionally I'd hear a child shouting in glee or a girl screeching in the midst of the inevitable boys-chasing-the-girls routine. However, it didn't hit home until night fell. The boys left, and the girls moved to the bedroom for a slumber party. Unfortunately the bedroom in which they were sleeping over was directly across from my bedroom. Not ten yards separated me from the joy I wasn't to be a part of. It was pitch-black outside, a spring night with windows flung open. I turned out all the lights in my room and pressed my nose against the window screen. I dared not breathe as I watched their every move shining out through the darkness. Tears streamed down my face, and in the loneliness of that moment, I took rejection as my lifelong companion. I became its slave; it became my master.

A few months later my master took me deeper into the dungeon. I decided to take revenge on the neighbor by throwing a swimming party to which everyone in the class—but her—would be invited. I had a saxophone lesson in the morning, and as I walked home dragging the heavy instrument case behind me, my heart was heavy too. I knew the idea was cruel, but she'd done it to me first. I pushed sympathy aside and got busy setting up in the backyard. I covered a little table with a paper cloth and set out some pretzels and potato chips. Then I sat down to wait for the party to begin.

It never did.

No one came. No one.

Of all the things I've lived in bondage to (I'll share more about those in the coming days), nothing has been more powerful than the feeling of being rejected. How I praise God that the message of the Cross is "No more condemnation" (Romans 8:1). No more rejection. No more "little girl no one is allowed to play with." How I praise God for the truth that I am 100 percent accepted in Christ and that I'm invited to the party.

Of course, discovering that truth is one thing, working it into your daily life is quite another. If you feel like you're on the outside looking in, like you haven't been invited to the party, if you're not living in the light of God's acceptance, but are in bondage to the past or to other people's opinions of you, then stick with me. Together we're gonna learn how to live every day in absolute freedom.

Reflections Along the Journey

1. Have you lived in bondage to rejection or to the fear of being rejected? Describe.

2. Have you had a life experience that left you feeling like you were on the outside looking in? Like you hadn't been invited to the party? If so, describe.

3. Write out a prayer thanking God for inviting you to the party.

4. What key lesson did you glean from today's study?

Freedom Truths:

- The message of the Cross is no more rejection.
- Discovering a truth is one thing; working that truth into your daily life is quite another.

Day Four

Escape and Recapture

Yesterday I shared how my world was turned upside down when my oldest brother returned from Vietnam addicted to heroin. Now for the real irony. After seeing the human carnage and the wreckage of drugs, after seeing them tear my family apart and rob me of my childhood, guess what I became? When the Hound of Heaven tracked me down and dragged me kicking and screaming into the kingdom of God, I was not only a drug addict, I was a drug dealer. I was so enslaved to drugs that I became the kind of scum who would give your kid free drugs just to get him hooked and land a long-term customer.

But I praise God that he did not leave me in that place. In July 1980 I received a phone call from a high school friend who invited me to go on a vacation in northern Pennsylvania. He said the setting was breathtaking and the people were fabulous—and it started the following day. He concluded the conversation by saying, "I'm paying your way, so you can't say no. I'm picking you up tomorrow at 5:00 A.M."

I hung up the phone and figured, *Hey, what have I got to lose? It's a free vacation*. I quickly packed my bags, including my string bikini and a couple of joints (that's marijuana cigarettes, for the uninitiated). Boy, was I in for a big surprise when we pulled into the Presbyterian Retreat Center. Of course, I wasn't nearly as surprised as the camp directors were when they saw me!

For the first couple of days I argued with them and generally made their lives miserable. Then one day I was sitting on the bank of the Delaware River when it suddenly became real to me: Even if I were the only person on the planet, Jesus Christ would have gone to the cross to pay the price for my sins. I was filled with an inexpressible joy. From that moment on I've never had a single craving for drugs.

And that from a person who literally could not make it until ten in the morning without getting high. Talk about being set free!

The next night there was a beautiful moon in the sky. As I walked along the river gazing at the wonder of God's creation, I heard him speak to me in a way that was so clear it was like he was walking next to me. He said, *"I'm going to take you to retreat centers just like this one all over the country. And I'm going to use you in a mighty way to make a difference in this world."*

I was so excited I thought I would burst! I had been set free, and I was ready to lead my fellow slaves to freedom. After all, I knew John 3:16. I figured it would take me a couple of months to get a handle on the Bible, a few more months to get my name out, and I'd be speaking at retreat centers before you could say hermeneutics! To tell you the truth, by the end of the week I was ready to say to the guy teaching the camp, "You can sit down. I'll take it from here."

I can assure you, it didn't quite work out that way.

Two months after my moonlight encounter with God, I went off to college. During the first week I met a young Iranian man who was to change my life forever. I had grown up in a home that was out of control. Believe me, when you have four heroin addicts, you have a world that's out of control. So when I met this young man, I thought, *Now here is someone who has got things under control. Here's someone who can help me get my life under control too.*

Did he get my life under control?

Oh my!

This was in the midst of the Iranian Hostage Crisis. Little did I know I was about to endure an Iranian hostage crisis of my own. For the next ten years I was not allowed to leave my house unsupervised.[4] I was not allowed to drive. I was not allowed to go to a grocery store, not even to the corner convenience store to pick up a bottle of milk. I don't want to get bogged down in details here. Let me just put it this way: My husband exerted total control over my life.

One Saturday morning stands out in my mind. I woke up to an absolutely glorious day—a rarity in New Jersey—and I wanted so much to go for a walk around the block. Of course, such activities

---

[4]The ten years span two years of dating and engagement and our first eight years of marriage. Initially I thought he was just extremely attentive, and that is the way I tried to portray him to those around us.

were completely forbidden, but I thought maybe, just maybe, this once. I remember cautiously asking my husband. The answer was no. So I asked, *"Can I at least sit on the front steps?"* The answer was no.

I can remember during those years tormenting myself, *God, didn't you say what I thought you said? I mean, the one time I actually heard a voice from heaven, and I got the message wrong? How am I going to travel around the country when I can't even walk around the block? How is all this gonna work out, Lord?*

I couldn't help wondering what on earth had happened to my life. Having been set free, having escaped the bondage of drugs, I had somehow allowed myself to be recaptured. Now I was in bondage to my husband's Middle Eastern value system.

Why couldn't the God who had instantly set me free from drugs just as quickly set me free from my Iranian captivity? I realize now that God was trying to set me free the whole time, but since it wasn't the type of freedom I was looking for, I didn't recognize it when it came. I now realize that before God could set me free *from* my circumstances, he wanted me to learn how to be set free *in the midst of* my circumstances. The lessons I have learned during that process form the substance of this book.

Do you know what it is to live in bondage? Have you made choices that have enslaved you? Perhaps you've become enslaved to a bad habit: smoking, drinking, diet pills, soap operas, overeating, gossip, a negative attitude. Perhaps you've become enslaved by another person's choices: your husband's career (low pay, long hours, frequent travel), your child's failures, your boss's work ethics. Have you been asking God to deliver you *from* your circumstances rather than deliver you *in the midst of* your circumstances? It's possible that God doesn't want to change your circumstances; he just wants to change you. It's also possible that *after* God changes you, he will change your circumstances too!

Reflections Along the Journey

1. Recall where you were when the Hound of Heaven tracked *you* down. Spend a few moments thanking him for his mercy to you.

2. Can you think of any choices you have made that have enslaved you?

3. Has someone in your life made choices by which you feel enslaved?

4. List some ways that God might set you free in the midst of your circumstances.

5. Write out a prayer thanking God for his deliverance.

6. What key lesson did you glean from today's study?

Freedom Truths:

- Even as Christians, we can become enslaved by our own foolish choices.
- Rather than deliver you *from* your circumstances, God may deliver you *in the midst of* your circumstances.

Day Five

The Drift Toward Slavery

S ome people are seized quickly and dragged away as slaves. That's what happened to Joseph, as you may recall. (If you are not familiar with this story, we'll get to it soon enough). However, most of us wake up one morning and realize that step by step we've been led into bondage. We've been seduced by false promises, and by the time we realize we've been tricked, it's too late to walk away without a battle.

Here's how Joseph's brothers were seduced into taking the first step toward slavery:

> When the news reached Pharaoh's palace that Joseph's brothers had come, Pharaoh and all his officials were pleased. Pharaoh said to Joseph, "Tell your brothers, 'Do this: Load your animals and return to the land of Canaan, and bring your father and your families back to me. I will give you the best of the land of Egypt and you can enjoy the fat of the land.' You are also directed to tell them, 'Do this: Take some carts from Egypt for your children and your wives, and get your father and come. Never mind about your belongings, because the best of all Egypt will be yours.' So the sons of Israel did this" (Genesis 45:16–21a).

It all starts so wonderfully, doesn't it? The kind Pharaoh, impressed with Joseph, invites his whole family to come down to Egypt. "Come unto me," he says. "I'll take care of you. Don't worry about a thing." Joseph's family, the Israelites, have great expectations as they walk confidently into Egypt, ready to enjoy the best of everything.

If we didn't know the end of this story, we never would have guessed it closes with four hundred years of slavery. God allowed the Israelites to travel down to Egypt, but *they* allowed Egypt into their hearts. Egypt promised them the best but gave them the worst. Egypt promised freedom but enslaved them instead. God wanted them to live among the Egyptians for a season, not to take up permanent dwelling there.

In the same way, God has sent us into the world, but we are not to allow the world into our hearts:

> I have given them your word and the world has hated them, for they are not of the world any more than I am of the world. My prayer is not that you take them out of the world but that you protect them from the evil one. They are not of the world, even as I am not of it. Sanctify them by the truth; your word is truth. As you sent me into the world, I have sent them into the world. For them I sanctify myself, that they too may be truly sanctified. (John 17:14–18)

The world is not our permanent dwelling place; we're only here for a season. When we lose sight of that truth, we end up enslaved to the world's false promises. We become seduced by our culture, eager to get our hands on the best this world has to offer. We even hear preachers declare that the abundant life Christ promises consists of beautiful homes and new cars. As a result, the average Christian family is virtually indistinguishable from their heathen neighbors.

Jesus said the only way to live in Egypt without becoming enslaved is to be sanctified by the truth. Sanctify means "to set apart as sacred, consecrate, *to make free from sin*, purify."[5] And how are we made free from sin? Through his Word, the Bible.

The first step on your personal journey to living in absolute freedom is *facing your bondage*. It begins when you realize that although the promises of our culture sound wonderful, you are in constant danger of being enslaved. It also means coming to grips with the areas of your life in which you've given ground to those thoughts, ideas, people, and things that would enslave you. We've already begun this process during the first week of our study, and we'll continue throughout the second and third weeks.

Once you've faced your bondage, you're ready to *receive your deliverer*. When Pharaoh offers, "Come unto me. I'll give you the best of the land," you must resist, turning instead to the one who said, "Come

---

[5]*Webster's Dictionary* (emphasis added).

to *me*. For my yoke is easy and my burden is light" (Matthew 11:28, 30). Week 4 will help you *open your heart* to the only One who can truly deliver you.

Week 5 will offer practical steps to help you *embrace your liberty*, demonstrating how you can liberate your heart, mind, and will.

Weeks 6 and 7 will help you *emancipate your fellow slaves* as you learn not only to forgive but also to transform the broken places in your life into avenues of ministry.

During Week 8, you'll discover how to *delight yourself in God* rather than looking to people, places, or things to delight you.

Week 9 will enable you to *overcome pockets of resistance*, those areas of your life that have previously seemed impervious to all your prayers and New Year's resolutions.

Week 10, our final week, will empower and energize you to *move forward in absolute freedom*.

I wish you Godspeed on your journey!

Reflections Along the Journey

1. How did Joseph's descendants become enslaved?

2. Can you see any parallels in your own life (i.e., have you responded to promises of "the best" this world has to offer)?

3. What is the *only* way to live in "Egypt" without becoming enslaved?

4. Write out a prayer asking God's guidance as you undertake this journey.

5. What key lesson did you glean from today's study?

6. Write out this week's verse from memory.

Freedom Truths:

- The only way to live in Egypt without becoming enslaved is to be sanctified by the truth.
- Beware of anyone who invites you to "come unto" them, promising you the best this world has to offer.

Weekly Review:

See if you can fill in the seven steps toward living in absolute freedom. Look in the back of the book if you need help.

F _____ your bondage

R _____ your Deliverer

E _____ your liberty

E _____ your fellow slaves

D _____ yourself in God

O _____ pockets of resistance

M _____ forward in absolute freedom

WEEK TWO:

Face Your Bondage, Part Two
Legalism Versus License

This Week's Verse:

Live as free men, but do not use your freedom as a cover-up
for evil; live as servants of God.

1 Peter 2:16

Day One

Slaves to Sin

*What a wretched man I am! Who will rescue me from this body
of death? Thanks be to God—through Jesus Christ our Lord!*
Romans 7:24–25

I need to warn you up front: this is not a fun week. We're going
to grapple with some of the most complex passages in the entire New
Testament, and we're going to delve into the most divisive issues facing the church today. I want to ask you to *stick with me*. Those of you
who have completed *Becoming a Vessel God Can Use* or *Walking in
Total God-Confidence* will probably wonder what happened to your old
pal Donna. I promise you, I'm still with you! I also promise that if you
will trudge through this tough terrain with me, we're gonna crash
through to a whole new level of spiritual growth on this journey. OK,
here we go.

I kept trying to think of a way to get around throwing out this
verse during the second week of our study. I can just see you all
scratching your heads, then tossing this book across the bathroom
floor, never to be read again. (What? You're not reading this in the
bathroom? You're in the minority!)

Anyway, no matter how convoluted, here it comes:

I am unspiritual, sold as a slave to sin. I do not understand
what I do. For what I want to do I do not do, but what I hate I
do. And if I do what I do not want to do, I agree that the law is
good. As it is, it is no longer I myself who do it, but it is sin living
in me. I know that nothing good lives in me, that is, in my sinful
nature. For I have the desire to do what is good, but I cannot
carry it out. For what I do is not the good I want to do; no, the
evil I do not want to do—this I keep on doing. Now if I do what

I do not want to do, it is no longer I who do it, but it is sin living in me that does it.

So I find this law at work: When I want to do good, evil is right there with me. For in my inner being I delight in God's law; but I see another law at work in the members of my body, waging war against the law of my mind and making me a prisoner of the law of sin at work within my members. What a wretched man I am! Who will rescue me from this body of death? Thanks be to God—through Jesus Christ our Lord!

So then, I myself in my mind am a slave to God's law, but in the sinful nature a slave to the law of sin. (Romans 7:14–25)

So, clear as mud, huh? Let's take another look at this passage, this time from *The Living Bible* paraphrase:

The law is good, then, and the trouble is not there but with *me* because I am sold into slavery with Sin as my owner. I don't understand myself at all, for I really want to do what is right, but I can't. I do what I don't want to—what I hate. I know perfectly well that what I am doing is wrong, and my bad conscience proves that I agree with these laws I am breaking. But I can't help myself, because I'm no longer doing it. It is sin inside me that is stronger than I am that makes me do these evil things.

I know I am rotten through and through so far as my old sinful nature is concerned. No matter which way I turn I can't make myself do right. I want to but I can't. When I want to do good, I don't; and when I try not to do wrong, I do it anyway. Now if I am doing what I don't want to, it is plain where the trouble is: sin still has me in its evil grasp.

It seems to be a fact of life that when I want to do what is right, I inevitably do what is wrong. I love to do God's will so far as my new nature is concerned; but there is something else deep within me, in my lower nature, that is at war with my mind and wins the fight and makes me a slave to the sin that is still within me. In my mind I want to be God's willing servant but instead I find myself still enslaved to sin.

So you see how it is: my new life tells me to do right, but the old nature that is still inside me loves to sin. Oh, what a terrible predicament I'm in! Who will free me from my slavery to this deadly lower nature? Thank God! It has been done by Jesus Christ our Lord. He has set me free. (Romans 7:14–25 TLB)

So what on earth does all this mean? Today we get to cover what I call the three-i-fications. (I made that word up to help my then-twelve-year-old daughter remember these three vitally important theological concepts. Sorta catchy, huh?) Let me give you my non-theologian's theological perspective: Positionally, in Christ, we have been declared completely holy. We've been set free from the power of sin to destroy us. When God looks upon us, he doesn't see our sin, but Christ's sinless life. That's *justification*.

Someday when we stand before God we will, *in fact*, be sinless. We will have perfect minds and hearts—even our bodies will be perfect. No more fat thighs for me. Yippee!!! That's called *glorification*.

Meanwhile we're stuck here on earth. I've got fat thighs, bad hair, and, not infrequently, a crummy attitude. But, hey, I'm working on it. Well, at least on *some days*. The process by which God takes us from where we are, namely *emancipated but still living on the plantation, thinking and acting like a slave*, to becoming increasingly free from the cares of this world—and, therefore, increasingly conformed to the character of Christ, is called *sanctification*. (Boy, that was a long sentence!)

Jesus has taken care of the *justification*—he paid the price on the cross so that we might be declared free from sin. The Father will take care of the glorification when the time is right: "We shall be like him for we shall see him as he is" (1 John 3:2). And the Holy Spirit stands ready to assist us in the process of sanctification. Did you notice the Trinity at work in the three-i-fications?

However, many Christians don't seem to understand that *we must participate in this process*. Yes, we are saved by grace. But as the Puritans were fond of saying, we must "avail ourselves of the means of grace" if we are to make progress in our journey toward holiness. By "means of grace" they meant spiritual disciplines, such as Bible study, prayer, meditation, attendance at public worship.

The more practical holiness we work into our daily lives, the more freedom we will enjoy. It should be obvious that the less mastery sin has over us, the more free we will become to do and be all that God is calling us to do and be. When you really think about it, absolute freedom is just another term for holiness. Jerry Bridges (my favorite contemporary author, for those who wonder about such things) has said, "An understanding of how grace and personal, vigorous effort work together is essential for a lifelong pursuit of holiness."[1]

I couldn't agree more, and I trust you'll agree, too, before this journey is over.

Reflections Along the Journey

1. What is justification?

2. What is glorification?

3. What is sanctification?

4. Can you think of some practical ways that you might "avail yourself of the means of grace"?

5. Write out a prayer expressing your desire to grow in sanctification.

---

[1]Jerry Bridges, *The Discipline of Grace: God's Role and Our Role in the Pursuit of Holiness* (Colorado Springs: NavPress, 1994), 13.

6. What key lesson did you glean from today's study?

Freedom Truths:

- Christ paid the price that we might be declared free from sin—that's justification.
- Someday, when we stand before the Father, we will be set eternally free from the power of sin—that's glorification.
- Meanwhile, the Holy Spirit stands ready to assist us as we struggle to break free from the power of sin, here and now—that's sanctification.

Day Two

Legalism Versus License

I begin with a tale of two churches. The tales are based in truth, though slightly fictionalized. It's Sunday morning, which doesn't mean much to sixteen-year-old Krista. She never went to church growing up, but lately she's been asking questions. Her father died three years ago on Christmas Day, and she's struggling to make sense of it all. Several weeks ago a friend invited her to a small youth retreat, and it was there that Krista asked Jesus into her heart. She knows what happened to her was real, but the people who hosted the retreat live two hours away and she's not sure what to do next.

She can't seem to make sense of the Bible they gave her, and even though she vowed to change, she's been out partying with her old friends again. Last night she got "totally wasted" and started throwing up. It scared her to think her drinking could get so out of control. Her dad was an alcoholic; that's why he died. She doesn't want to end up like him.

She woke up early this morning determined to go to church. But where? She remembered the church on Main Street. *That should be good*, she thought. So she stumbles out of bed, throws on some clothes, and gets her mom to drop her off at the church. She's nervous, but remembers the people at the retreat had been so friendly. She felt close to them right away. She hoped it would be the same here.

Krista walks into the church and looks around cautiously. Time drags. Finally a middle-aged woman heads toward her. Krista smiles. The woman doesn't. "I'm sorry, young lady. You'll have to go home and change. We do not allow women to wear pants in this church."

Krista stands there—speechless.

She leaves, and hasn't been to church since.

Devin never went to church growing up, either. But three years ago a friend from school invited him to his youth group and it was totally awesome. Now he never misses: if the church doors are open, Devin's there. Why not? The girls in the youth group are hot. He had the idea that religious girls were supposed to dress a certain way, but not these girls. They show it all—on purpose. It's like they sit around thinking up excuses to bend over.

Of course, the best part of church is the games. They always play rough games that give Devin the perfect excuse to grab the girls pretty much wherever he likes. No one says anything. Or they play games like "Pass the Donut," from his mouth to hers. One night they played a game where the guys put potato chips covered with Cheez Whiz in their mouths. The girls had to lick off the cheese. It really turned him on. Afterward he "made out" with the pastor's daughter in one of the Sunday school rooms. It was pretty intense. He knows it's just a matter of time before they have sex. She's already slept with a few of the guys in the youth group. Everybody is into who's dating who and who's sleeping with whom. That's basically the main topic of conversation.

Yeah, and the youth pastor is totally cool too. He knows Devin gets high before youth group every Wednesday night, but he doesn't seem to mind. Everyone knows there's a bunch of kids behind the church smoking pot before it starts. One time Devin heard someone's mom giving the youth pastor a hard time about it, but he just said something like "We're reaching the unchurched" and "We have to meet people where they are." Whatever that means.

Every once in a while the youth pastor starts "getting religious," but it's no big deal. It's not enough to ruin anything. Yeah, youth group is great.

There you have it. Two churches: one so legalistic it turns away an orphan, one so bent on being relevant that it has been transformed into a nightclub. By the way, if I told you how much of that fictional tale was actually nonfiction, you'd be shocked. Now I'll tell you something even more shocking: the root problem in both cases is—get ready for this—theology. Theology? Yep, theology.

I'm continually amazed at the number of people—even respected Bible teachers—who mishandle the Word of God in the area of justification versus sanctification. They tend to fall into two distinct camps: The first are those who overlook the significance of our justification—our secure position in Christ—and become obsessed with the pursuit of sanctification. Their Christianity then becomes performance oriented and legalistic. In the earlier decades of the twentieth century, legalism reigned supreme: women couldn't wear pants, men couldn't have the occasional bottle of beer, no self-respecting Christian would be caught dead in a movie theater, that sort of thing. Great emphasis was placed on outward conformity with little concern for the inward reality and *no* concern for love or mercy toward those who didn't measure up to the church's exacting standards. (We'll talk more about legalism a bit later.)

The second camp, more common in the church today, are those who use verses about our justification to obliterate the need for our active participation in sanctification. The result is license and worldliness. When I hear that the teen pregnancy rate among kids attending the local evangelical church is actually *higher* than the teen pregnancy rate for the general population; when I meet Christians in business who are *less* ethical, *less* reliable than their non-Christian counterparts; when I meet Christian men who'd rather play golf than attend church, Christian women who'd rather attend aerobics class than a weekly Bible study, and Christian children who know more about professional athletes than they do about Bible characters, I know that something is out of balance in the church today.

We preach grace, grace, and more grace. We preach the effectiveness of the Cross, that Christ has done it all. We should preach such messages, because it's true: positionally, Christ has done it all. We are completely free in Christ, but we often fail to mention that "a man is a slave to whatever has mastered him" (2 Peter 2:19b).

As we study passages from the Word of God, let's be sure to keep them in context. Is the passage addressing our position? Is it a truth to claim? To be more theological about it, does it refer to our justification? Or is it addressing our *journey*? Is it a lifestyle to pursue? Back to the theological term: is it written in regard to our sanctification?

This may sound like I'm playing with words or quibbling over minor details. I'm not. You may be thinking, *Gee, Donna, I thought you wrote* practical *books. This stuff doesn't seem very practical!* Trust me. You will see in time that it is immensely practical and that your understanding of these truths will have a profound impact on the way you live. As A. W. Tozer put it: "Because we are the handiwork of God, it follows that *all of our problems and their solutions are theolog-*

ical. Some knowledge of what kind of God it is that operates the universe is indispensable to a sound philosophy of life and a sane outlook on the world."[2]

Our goal in the next few days (and, indeed, throughout this study) will be to discover the balance. How we can live in absolute freedom, unfettered by the man-made rules of legalism, without abusing our freedom—that is, without giving way to license.

Where are you standing in that balance?

Reflections Along the Journey

1. What type of people do we become when we overlook the importance of our justification and focus on sanctification?

2. What type of people do we become when we overlook the importance of our sanctification and stand solely on our justification?

3. Do you tend toward legalism? Or license? Explain your answer.

---

[2]A. W. Tozer, *Knowledge of the Holy* (Harper San Francisco, 1992), 27.

4. Can you see how mishandling the Word of God concerning sanctification vs. justification has led you to be out of balance?

5. Write out a prayer, asking God to give you balance: that you would
be a believer who stands confident in her justification, yet daily
yields her life to the process of sanctification.

6. What key lesson did you glean from today's study?

Freedom Truths:

- When we overlook the significance of our justification, we become
legalistic.
- When we overlook the importance of our sanctification, we
become worldly.

Day Three

Enslaved by Legalism

Such regulations indeed have an appearance of wisdom, with their self-imposed worship, their false humility and their harsh treatment of the body, but they lack any value in restraining sensual indulgence.

Colossians 2:23

These two camps—the legalists and the licentious—aren't new. The apostle Paul addressed them both during the first century. First, let's see what he has to say to the legalists:

Therefore do not let anyone judge you by what you eat or drink, or with regard to a religious festival, a New Moon celebration or a Sabbath day. These are a shadow of the things that were to come; the reality, however, is found in Christ. Do not let anyone who delights in false humility and the worship of angels disqualify you for the prize. Such a person goes into great detail about what he has seen, and his unspiritual mind puffs him up with idle notions. He has lost connection with the Head, from whom the whole body, supported and held together by its ligaments and sinews, grows as God causes it to grow.

Since you died with Christ to the basic principles of this world, why, as though you still belonged to it, do you submit to its rules: "Do not handle! Do not taste! Do not touch!"? These are all destined to perish with use, because they are based on human commands and teachings. Such regulations indeed have an appearance of wisdom, with their self-imposed worship, their false humility and their harsh treatment of the body, but they lack any value in restraining sensual indulgence. (Colossians 2:16–23)

Frankly, I'm not even sure what to add to the above passage. It clearly leaves no room for legalism, and yet many Christians are enslaved to rules of one sort or another. I realize I'm treading on very dangerous territory here; some of you may be offended. That's not my purpose. My purpose is to call you to the freedom Christ offers.

I came to know Christ through the ministry of a denomination that was quite legalistic. I'll never forget when the young man who led me to Christ got up in front of our church to play a contemporary Christian song on an acoustic guitar. It was a very mild Steve Green song. Nevertheless, thirty families walked out of the service and never came back. I'm talking about folks who say, "If the *Trinity Hymnal* and an old organ were good enough for Jesus, they're good enough for me." I call that legalism run amok. (For those who haven't brushed up on their church history lately, neither organs nor the *Trinity Hymnal* existed when Jesus walked the earth.)

Throughout my college years I can remember living in torment on Sundays. While the other students were catching up on their reports or preparing for exams, I would be pacing my dorm room, wringing my hands, terrified to study in violation of the Sabbath but FAR from entering into the Sabbath rest Christ spoke of. Shopping was strictly forbidden on the Sabbath, and I specifically remember a sermon condemning Christians who went out together for lunch after the service.

Now, don't get me wrong. I still believe that observing a Sabbath—setting aside one day per week to focus on our spiritual lives—is a wonderful principle. However, we are not constrained by Old Testament restrictions because Christ himself *is* our Sabbath rest (Hebrews 4:1–16). It is in him, daily, that we receive spiritual refreshment. It is *to* him, daily, that we should withdraw from the cares of this world to find rest for our souls.

Why, then, was I letting others judge me based on my handling of a Sabbath day? The Colossians passage clearly states that we should not let anyone judge us with regard to a Sabbath day. By the same token, if you WANT to set apart a Sabbath day of rest, if it is a blessing to you, then by all means, go for it. Don't let me, or anyone else, judge you because of it. I believe we are free to celebrate it—or not celebrate it—according to our own convictions.

Then there are the so-called social sins, such as smoking, drinking, dancing, movies, and such. I have many precious friends, particularly in the homeschool movement, who follow spiritual leaders who have developed rules about *everything*: what music you can listen to, what movies you can and cannot watch, etc., etc., ad nauseum. If those guidelines are helpful to your Christian walk; if they draw you closer to God and enable you to live in greater unity with your fellow believers (those are, after all, the two greatest commandments), then I say, "Wonderful!" However, when these guidelines become a point of contention, when they cause division in the church, when they *enslave* rather than liberate you, they are no longer principles; they are a virtual prison cell.

Bottom line: Principles are not more important than people. People are more important than principles. You can search the entire gospel record and you will not find a single instance where Jesus elevated principles above people. Indeed, this is the very thing he condemned the Pharisees for doing: "They tie up heavy loads and put them on men's shoulders, but they themselves are not willing to lift a finger to move them" (Matthew 23:4).

Lately I've been privileged to speak for a number of Worldwide Church of God congregations. This church was formerly cultic in its practices. In fact, you will find it included in most books written on modern cults.[3] However, an amazing thing has happened since the death of this church's former leader: they've discovered the gospel of grace.

It's been one of the greatest joys of my life to hear these brothers and sisters share the incredible FREEDOM they've discovered. Formerly they lived enslaved to all kinds of rules and regulations; now they are free in Christ. Perhaps the most tragic outcome of their former bondage is the rebellion of many of their young people. I recall one pastor in particular sharing how his own precious son had become addicted to heroin. He explained how the weight of the law became unbearable for many of the young people, so that they gave themselves over to unbridled license. Now their churches are prayerfully working to restore relationships destroyed by the chains of legalism.

It may seem ironic that legalism would lead to license, yet that is precisely what the Scriptures (Colossians 2) *warn* will happen: "Such

---

[3]For a look at the revival that has occurred in that church, see Appendix A in the new expanded edition of Walter Martin, *The Kingdom of the Cults* (Minneapolis: Bethany House Publishers, 1997). Also Joseph Tkach, *Transformed by Truth* (Sisters, Ore.: Multnomah Publishers, 1997) traces the incredible story of how this cult has now embraced historic Christianity.

regulations indeed have an appearance of wisdom, with their self-imposed worship, their false humility and their harsh treatment of the body, but they lack any value in restraining sensual indulgence." When we become consumed with outward rules and regulations, we neglect the *inward reality*.

God doesn't want outward conformity; he wants our hearts. He doesn't want our conduct controlled by rules and regulations; he wants our conduct controlled by *love*. We'll explore that idea more on Day Five. Tomorrow we get to pick on the licentious.

Reflections Along the Journey

1. So did I step on your toes today? How so?

2. Are you in any way enslaved to legalism?

3. Write out a prayer expressing your desire to be motivated by your *love of God* rather than by the law.

4. What key lesson did you glean from today's study?

Freedom Truths:

- Do not let anyone judge you based on your adherence to legalistic rules and regulations.
- The relentless pursuit of legalistic ideals can actually lead to license.

Day Four

Enslaved by License

What shall we say, then? Shall we go on sinning so that grace may increase? By no means! We died to sin; how can we live in it any longer?

Romans 6:1–2

Yesterday some of you were thinking, *You go, Donna. Give it to all those stodgy, self-righteous legalists! I always knew they had it all wrong. Not me, I'm free in Christ. I can do whatever I feel like doing. I just claim 1 John 1:9 afterwards and, hey, no problem!*

Well, Paul has some pointed words for y'all as well:

> Those who live according to the sinful nature have their minds set on what that nature desires; but those who live in accordance with the Spirit have their minds set on what the Spirit desires. The mind of sinful man is death, but the mind controlled by the Spirit is life and peace; the sinful mind is hostile to God. It does not submit to God's law, nor can it do so. Those controlled by the sinful nature cannot please God.
>
> You, however, are controlled not by the sinful nature but by the Spirit, if the Spirit of God lives in you. And if anyone does not have the Spirit of Christ, he does not belong to Christ. But if Christ is in you, your body is dead because of sin, yet your spirit is alive because of righteousness. (Romans 8:5–10)

No question about it. In the church, the pendulum has swung full course *away* from legalism and toward license. In many cases we've overreacted to the dry dogma and dead ritual of the old denominations to the extent that the average American Christian is literally indistinguishable from his pagan counterpart. My friends, this should not be so: "Shall we go on sinning so that grace may increase? By no means! We died to sin; how can we live in it any longer?" (Romans 6: 1–2).

Christ calls us to be a holy people. The word "holy" literally means "peculiar" or "set apart." Here's a test you can give yourself to discover if you are erring on the side of license: How much of your lifestyle would your neighbors label "peculiar"?

Maybe you drive an old sedan when you could afford a new mini-van, because you'd rather send the money to missionaries than to the Ford Motor Company credit department. Maybe you're a one-income family in a two-income world. Maybe you make tremendous lifestyle sacrifices to keep your children in Christian school. Maybe your teen-agers spend their summers on short-term mission trips rather than working on their suntans.

Then again, maybe your family fits in perfectly.

If there is *nothing* peculiar about your lifestyle, my guess is that you are living on the side of license. Yes, you are free to have a brand-new car. Yes, you are free to have your children in public school. Yes, both parents are free to work outside the home. I won't comment on the suntans.

I'm not talking about your freedom; I'm talking about your *choices*. " 'Everything is permissible for me'—but not everything is beneficial. 'Everything is permissible for me'—but I will not be mastered by any-thing" (1 Corinthians 6:12).

I am free to watch R-rated movies, but are they beneficial to me? Does my doing so line up with Philippians 4:8: "Finally, brothers, whatever is true, whatever is noble, whatever is right, whatever is pure, whatever is lovely, whatever is admirable—if anything is excel-lent or praiseworthy—think about such things"?

I am free to shuffle my kids from one sporting event to the next, keeping them so busy they couldn't read their Bibles if they wanted to. But is it beneficial to them? Does it line up with Ephesians 6:4, where fathers in particular are instructed to "bring them [their chil-dren] up in the training and instruction of the Lord"?

I am free to smoke, drink, and eat junk food all day. But are these things beneficial? Do they line up with 1 Corinthians 6:19–20: "Do you not know that your body is a temple of the Holy Spirit, who is in you, whom you have received from God? You are not your own; you were bought at a price. Therefore honor God with your body"?

Do any of these, and a thousand other things we are "free" to do, line up with Colossians 3:2–10?

> Set your minds on things above, not on earthly things. For you died, and your life is now hidden with Christ in God. When Christ, who is your life, appears, then you also will appear with him in glory.
>
> Put to death, therefore, whatever belongs to your earthly nature: sexual immorality, impurity, lust, evil desires and greed, which is idolatry. Because of these, the wrath of God is coming. You used to walk in these ways, in the life you once lived. But now you must rid yourselves of all such things as these: anger, rage, malice, slander, and filthy language from your lips. Do not lie to each other, since you have taken off your old self with its practices and have put on the new self, which is being renewed in knowledge in the image of its Creator.

Yes, we are free to make our own choices, but let us never forget: first we make our choices, then our choices make us. Invariably those verses in Scripture that proclaim our freedom simultaneously warn us of the law of choice and consequences, as A. W. Tozer called it. This truth is absolutely critical to understanding and living out our freedom:

> Whoever is on God's side [the side of righteous living] is on the winning side and cannot lose; whoever is on the other side is on the losing side and cannot win. Here there is no chance, no gamble. There is freedom to choose which side we shall be on but no freedom to negotiate the results of the choice once it is made. By the mercy of God we may repent a wrong choice and alter the consequences by making a new and right choice.[4]

The next time you are exulting in the truth that you are free to make your own choices, remember: You are not free from the consequences of those choices.

Reflections Along the Journey

1. How is your life distinguishable from your non-Christian neighbors?

---

[4]A. W. Tozer, 112.

2. What are some consequences you have reaped by erring on the side of license?

3. Write out a prayer asking God to deliver you from the chains of license.

4. What key lesson did you glean from today's study?

Freedom Truths:

- If our lives are indistinguishable from our non-Christian neighbors, we are probably erring on the side of license.
- We are free to make our own choices, but we are not free from the consequences of those choices.

Day Five

Liberty

Live as free men, but do not use your freedom as a cover-up for evil; live as servants of God.

1 Peter 2:16

Leave it to Peter to get right to the point. Paul, bless his heart, has dragged us kicking and screaming through four days of elaborate theological treatises featuring convoluted logic and sentences that run on for pages. Here, everyone's favorite fisherman narrows it down to a single sentence. You gotta love this guy!

To all of us, he says, "Live as free men."

To the licentious, he warns, "Do not use your freedom as a cover-up for evil."

To the legalist, he implores, "Live as servants of God." (Remember, servants don't tell everyone else what to do.)

Here, then, is the picture of the truly free Christian: the one who is controlled neither by legalism nor license but instead walks in liberty. When we walk in liberty, the only reason we do or do not do *anything* is simple: "For Christ's love compels us" (2 Corinthians 5:14).

In my diatribe on legalism I implied that the *Trinity Hymnal* is not the *only* approved songbook in God's eyes and that there are other appropriate instruments of praise aside from the organ. Having said that, I will hasten to add that I am deeply alarmed at the way many churches have casually tossed aside the great hymns of the faith. Now, here's how seriously I hold that conviction: My daughter Leah takes piano lessons for the *express purpose* of learning hymns and keeping them alive for the next generation. If you look in her piano bench, you'll find a large collection of hymnbooks, but no contemporary praise and worship songs.

54

Balance. That's what we're talking about here. Balance comes when we are compelled by the love of Christ—not by law or by what feels good or by what is convenient. Balance comes when we are compelled by deeply held convictions, derived not from our fellowmen but from the Word of God:

> To pursue holiness, one of the disciplines we must become skilled in is the development of Bible-based convictions. A conviction is a determinative belief: something you believe so strongly that it affects the way you live. Someone has observed that a belief is what you hold, but a conviction is what holds you. You may live contrary to what you believe, but you cannot live contrary to your convictions. This doesn't mean you never *act* contrary to your convictions, but that you do not consistently violate them. . . . We want to make sure our convictions are *Bible-based*, that they are *derived from our personal interaction with the Scriptures* [emphasis added].[5]

You can and should listen to sermons and audiotapes. You can and should read Christian books and attend seminars. But ultimately your convictions must be based not on someone else's opinions or someone else's understanding of the Scriptures but on your *own* study of God's Word. There's just no substitute. What do *you* believe? What is God revealing to you directly from his Word? How is he calling you to live?

To give you an example, through my personal study of Scripture and time alone before God, I became convicted that homeschooling is the right choice for our family. It's not just something I believe. It's not just that I think homeschooling is a nice alternative; I'm absolutely *convinced* to the point that I can't imagine any other option for our family. Now, I could turn it into a RULE and say, "Everyone better homeschool their children. Anyone who doesn't is a second-rate Christian." Does that demonstrate a servant's attitude? Instead, I live out my convictions and allow my brothers and sisters in Christ to live out theirs.

If you want to walk in liberty, live according to your own convictions and liberate your fellow believers to do likewise. Put another way, "Live as free men, but do not use your freedom as a cover-up for evil; live as servants of God" (1 Peter 2:16).

---

[5]Jerry Bridges, 58.

Reflections Along the Journey

1. What did you discover today (indeed, throughout this week) about the balance between legalism and license?

2. How can you begin to embrace a lifestyle of liberty?

3. Write out a prayer embracing liberty.

4. What key lesson did you glean from today's study?

5. Write out this week's verse from memory.

Freedom Truths:

- Live as free men, but do not use your freedom as a cover-up for evil.
- Live as servants of God.

Weekly Review:

See if you can fill in the seven steps toward living in absolute freedom. Look in the back of the book if you need help.

F _____ your bondage

R _____ your Deliverer

E _____ your liberty

E _____ your fellow slaves

D _____ yourself in God

O _____ pockets of resistance

M _____ forward in absolute freedom

WEEK THREE:

Face Your Bondage, Part Three
Sold Cheap

This Week's Verse:

I am he, I am he who will sustain you.
I have made you and I will carry you;
I will sustain you and I will rescue you.

Isaiah 46:4

Day One

Sold to Financial Security

For what shall it profit a man, if he shall gain the whole world, and lose his own soul?

Mark 8:36 KJV

I had a dream. First it terrified me. Then it changed my life.

The dream was set back in Philadelphia, where I lived and worked for many years. My husband and I were bustling about the house, suited up for another day of climbing the corporate ladder. We kept pushing past each other, grabbing this or that. No words were spoken.

The next scene found us jumping aboard the high-speed train to the office. Unexplainably our children turned up on the train with us. We paid little attention to them—or to each other. We were focused on the day to come and on the work that lay ahead. The loudspeaker called out our stop, and we, like a pair of robots on overdrive, joined the pushing and shoving as we dutifully exited the train amid the throng of businessmen and workingwomen. We headed off in two different directions. Then suddenly we stopped. We turned toward each other. Across the crowded train station our eyes met. Terror struck. We turned simultaneously toward the train just as the automatic doors were closing. We both screamed from the core of our being. But it was too late. The train had left the station *with our children on board*. We had left them behind, and now they were off to an unknown— and surely dangerous—destination without us.

Frantically we grabbed passersby, telling them of our dilemma and begging for help. No one shared our alarm. "They'll be fine," everyone assured us, walking away casually, as if we had lost our lunch bag. The policeman just shrugged his shoulders, even as I pulled on his blue starched shirt trying to shake him to his senses. We couldn't comprehend why no one else sensed the gravity of the situation. I began weeping uncontrollably.

Then I woke up.

Oh, Lord, don't let me lose my children, I pleaded in prayer. *Don't let me leave them behind. Don't let me be so consumed with my search for financial security that I lose all sense of perspective, that I lose sight of what matters most.*

God has been faithful in answering that prayer. Not by waving a magic wand that permanently changed my priorities, and certainly not by letting me win the lottery or gaining a great inheritance that would guarantee my financial security forever. Rather, he has led me little by little to make wise lifestyle choices. To the extent that I've opened my heart to his Holy Spirit, he has performed multiple surgeries to remove the many tumors, each filled with yearning for financial security, with the love of money.

We're talking about elective surgery here. You have to make the appointment and willingly submit to the procedure. No one's going to rush you to the emergency room. The people around you are oblivious to your symptoms; they don't even acknowledge that the disease exists. *No big deal,* they assure you. *Kids are resourceful. They'll find their way back home. After all, you're doing this for their sakes. They can understand that. You're not greedy. Your priorities aren't messed up. You just want financial security for your family. There's nothing wrong with that.*

Now maybe those of you who don't have children think you are off the hook on this one. Not so fast! I think you know it's entirely possible for a single person to sell herself cheap to financial security. And we all know about the DINKs. The acronym stands for Double Income, No Kids. I'm not saying that just because you are a DINK you have necessarily sold your soul to financial security. But let's face it, the DINKs are a symbol of that very phenomenon in our culture.

Examine your heart. See if the love of money has grown like a cancer there. If so, there's only one solution: radical surgery. Most people will think you're nuts for taking the risks and enduring the pain of such invasive surgery. It doesn't matter what other people think. Call the doctor: the Great Physician. Make an appointment.

Reflections Along the Journey

1. Have you become a slave to the pursuit of financial security?

2. In what ways has that pursuit caused you to leave your children—or others you love—behind?

3. Have you ever had a dream that had a profound impact on your life? Describe.

4. How did it change you?

5. Write out a prayer to The Great Physician, inviting him to surgically remove the love of money from your heart.

6. What key lesson did you glean from today's study?

Freedom Truths:

- Don't leave your family behind to pursue financial security.
- Allow God to remove the love of money from your heart.

Day Two

Sold to the Relentless Pursuit of Status

But I said, "I have labored to no purpose; I have spent my strength in vain and for nothing. Yet what is due me is in the Lord's hand, and my reward is with my God."

Isaiah 49:4

It's amazing how different people can do the exact same thing for very different reasons. Yesterday I shared how my husband and I were both on the fast train to the city. He was on the train in pursuit of financial security. I wanted that, too, but there was something else. Something more powerful, even more dangerous, than the love of money. Pride. Or to use a more polite term, the desire for status.

I spent the entire 1980s in the relentless pursuit of status. Maybe it was a 1980s thing. I don't meet as many women consumed with climbing the corporate ladder as I once did. Then again, maybe that's just because I now live in a Podunk town in the middle of nowhere. The only ladders around here are at the feed store. On the chance that there are still women out there expending themselves on the illusive goal of "having it all," I offer my experience as a word of warning.

Throughout the early years of my illustrious corporate career, I bore the title "secretary." No offense intended to secretaries, but to me it was a badge of humiliation. I, Donna Partow, who dreamed of attending Harvard my whole life (and who bragged to everyone about my dream). I, who had attended a ritzy Ivy League university (didn't graduate, just attended. Long story). I, who was going to be a famous corporate lawyer, sat in the midst of the go-go '80s earning five dollars an hour while my bosses (few of whom worked harder than me) raked in six figures.

I literally worked like a slave. I have shared previously that my husband, who is Iranian, would not let me leave the house unsupervised. However, since he was desperate for financial security—and hadn't been able to achieve it on his own—he let me go to work. My husband would drop me off in the morning before going to his office, which was usually an hour away. He'd work eight to ten hours, then pick me up at the end of the day. So right off the bat I was working an extra two to three hours a day, every day. If your math is better than mine, you've already figured out that I was averaging sixty hours per week. Since I wasn't allowed to go anywhere other than the office, and since I had no other way of boosting my nonexistent self-esteem, I worked. And I worked. And I worked. And when I work, LOOK OUT. I'm a one-woman working machine.

I worked frantically. Desperately. Hoping that someone would notice my drive, my talent, my commitment, and honor me with a new title. A prestigious title. I wanted to attend meetings with important people. I wanted status. I wanted a business card. I wanted a corner office. I wanted a company car. (I wasn't allowed to drive, so what was I thinking?)

Ironically, the more I sought it, the more it eluded me. Rather than noticing what a rare gem of an employee I was, most of my coworkers just thought I was a nut. A hyperactive, annoying nut at that.

Eventually God gave me a small taste of what I had yearned for. Gradually, rung by rung, I made my way up the corporate ladder. Finally, I was promoted to the prestigious Investment Banking department, where I sat in a huge cushy chair at a fabulous mahogany desk with brass fixtures. They printed my name on a business card with my fancy title emblazoned on it: Investment Banking Representative.

My new boss believed in me and wanted to send me out to win new customers.

Uh-oh.

Send me out? But, but, but—I wasn't allowed out!!! Of course, I didn't know how to tell my boss that. My first business trip was a trip, all right. They sent me to the bank's corporate headquarters in Pittsburgh. When I got to the hotel, guess who was waiting for me? Yep, my husband! He couldn't afford a plane ticket, so he spent all day riding the train. Is my life weird or what?

Ironically, the more freedom I won in the workplace, the tighter became my bondage at home. Then came the clincher. My boss promoted me again, and a company car came with the new position. *But I don't know how to drive*, I protested. *I'm afraid to drive.* I didn't have the guts to tell him I wasn't *allowed* to drive. Not one to put up with nonsense, he simply declared, "You WILL drive, or I'll fire you." So I learned to drive on the Schuylkill Expressway (better known as the Sure-Kill—you can guess why) with my boss at my side.

I took clients to fancy restaurants and did the round of prestigious corporate events. It wasn't all I thought it would be. Deep inside, I still felt like nothing. Like I'd never be anyone important.

I realized it wasn't the title; it was me.

About that time the ax fell. Remember the good ol' days of corporate downsizing? Our entire department was eliminated and told to clear out within the hour. My enslavement to corporate culture ended abruptly. But I was still enslaved to my yearning for status.

I realize my story is extreme. Nevertheless, I challenge you to examine your own heart. Is it possible that you've been living your life in the relentless pursuit of status? Is there a title, a badge of honor, you are desperate to earn? Do you feel an inordinate need to justify your existence? to prove that you are a worthwhile human being, that you *know* things, that you can *do* things, that you *count* for something?

I meet many young mothers who struggle with the title "stay-at-home mom." They feel like they need a job outside the home to feel important. Or they volunteer for committees or to coach the girls' softball team—anything that will give them a sense of significance. As I said, different people may do the same things for very different reasons. If you are active outside your home for the right reasons—and you can keep first things first—that's wonderful. However, if you are running away from the routine tasks of motherhood in search of status, you have sold yourself cheap. You are living in slavery. Christ wants to set you free.

Reflections Along the Journey

1. In what ways have you pursued status?

2. Are you pursuing activities outside the home for the wrong reasons?

3. Write out a prayer asking God to show you if you are enslaved to status.

4. What key lesson did you glean from today's study?

Freedom Truths:

- Different people can do exactly the same thing for very different reasons.
- As mothers, we must be careful not to run away from our homes in pursuit of status.

Day Three

Sold to the Status Quo

The images that are carried about are burdensome, a burden for the weary.

Isaiah 46:1

In describing the Israelites, Isaiah said they were burdened down by the idols, or images, they carried around. Although we don't think of ourselves as idol-worshipers, is it possible that you are carrying about images that are burdening you down? Perhaps they are images of the way you think life should be: more precisely, images of what you think your *lifestyle* should be.

I meet many people who are utterly enslaved to their image of the great American lifestyle. And those images have indeed become a burden for the weary:

- You have to have a college degree.
- You have to have a 2,500-square-foot house with a two-car garage.
- You have to eat out at least once a week.
- You have to have a professional haircut, and if you expect to count for anything you should invest in acrylic nails.
- You have to decorate and maintain a lovely home.
- You have to host tea parties. At the very least, you have to buy books about lovely tea parties and place them around the house.
- You have to learn to speed-clean.
- Your kids have to be well dressed—in store-bought clothes. And they need at least thirty sets of clothes to be normal.
- Your child will suffer emotional harm if you don't shop at the mall. Kmart clothes just don't cut it. Sneakers matter most.
- Your kids are entitled to Happy Meals and snow cones.
- You'd better be in line for every new Disney movie that comes out.

Any child with less than twenty-five videos in his personal collection is a neglected child.

- Your kids need to be involved in sports. Fortunately there's a sport for every season.
- If your child doesn't have at least twenty kids on her social calendar, she's deprived or abnormal. Throw a party, or take her for counseling. The important thing is, DO SOMETHING.

Are you exhausted yet?

A slave's life *IS* exhausting!

We're burdened down by images. All the stuff we accumulate, the status quo we pursue, become to us a burden for the weary. We need two incomes to keep up, so either Mom has to work or Dad has to work longer hours. It doesn't have to be that way. We don't have to live in bondage to the status quo. Money, possessions, and conformity cannot deliver us: "Though one cries out to it [riches and man-made idols], it does not answer; it cannot save him from his troubles" (Isaiah 46:7b).

The only one we can cry out to for deliverance is God. The only one who can save us from our troubles is God: "I am he, I am he who will sustain you. I have made you and I will carry you; I will sustain you and I will rescue you" (Isaiah 46:4b).

God can deliver us, he can rescue us, but we have to be willing to be rescued. Even when you've been rescued, it's hard to live in freedom when everyone around you is still in bondage. When we moved to Arizona in 1993, we discovered that the paltry profit from selling our 1,200-square-foot modular home in New Jersey was enough for a down payment on a beautiful house in a "planned community." (This was back in the old days when Arizona real estate was dirt cheap. And in case you're wondering, "planned community" means there's a golf course, tennis courts, and a swimming pool.)

I thought I had died and gone to heaven. Then reality began to sink in: I could afford the house, but affording the lifestyle was a whole different ball game.

Just to give you an example, there were birthday parties almost every week. That shouldn't be a big deal, right? It was. To me, a child's birthday party means cake and ice cream around the kitchen table. I soon found out that wasn't in keeping with the status quo. One birthday party featured pony rides, another had a petting zoo. Many parties were held in child-oriented restaurants: you know, the kind of place where a kid can be a kid. My personal favorite was the birthday party of a seven-year-old in which a limousine took all the little girls to the ballet.

Now, all this can be wonderful. But for me it became a form of slavery. When Leah's birthday rolled around, my life passed before me. How could I possibly keep up? I felt perpetually humiliated, inadequate, "less than."

Finally, God brought me to my senses. I think it was the day I was walking through the mall carrying a life-size Barbie doll. I had sworn I would never sink that low. Granted, Leah already had at least fifty Barbies, not to mention the Barbie kitchen, the Barbie swimming pool, and the Barbie convertible. I knew in my heart that the life-size Barbie was American decadence personified. But—well, what's a mother to do? "All" the other kids in the neighborhood were getting My Size Barbies. How could I deprive my child? Do you want to know the weirdest part? I don't even LIKE Barbie!

Don't get me wrong. If you can live in the midst of a planned community without becoming enslaved to the status quo, I think that's absolutely fabulous. You should stay there and be a light in the darkness. However, I never learned how to live in freedom on the "plantation." I had to leave the place of my enslavement in order to enter into true freedom. We moved to a small town in the mountains, where the kids play with goats and chickens rather than Barbies. I gave away all the Barbie stuff—except the $100 My Size Barbie. I just couldn't bring myself to get rid of it. I've kept it in storage for the last couple of years. Now, you won't believe this: yesterday my three-year-old, Taraneh, found the My Size Barbie, and it's sitting in the middle of my living room! UGH!

Are you enslaved to the status quo? You might have to do something radical, like leave the plantation.

I wrote the above lesson on a Saturday. The very next day we had a surprise visit from a family of ten who still lives in the midst of the "Barbie" neighborhood. The plantation lifestyle doesn't bother them in the least; they live and work in complete freedom in the midst of it. You can search their 2,800-square-foot house from top to bottom and you won't find a single Barbie.

On Monday yet another friend who still lives in the planned community dropped by. (We live in the middle of nowhere. Believe me, no one just "drops by." This was God at work.) We talked for hours about her life on the plantation. It never has and never will affect her value system. She told me an amusing story I must relate: her husband works on a medical rescue helicopter. He works forty-eight hours per week, but his schedule consists of two twenty-four-hour days with five days off. My friend said her husband is under constant pressure to get another job. A relative recently expressed concern because "he spends too much time with his children when he could be out making more money." We both shook our heads and laughed at the absurdity of that comment.

Sure, he could get another job and make more money. But why? They already have a comfortable lifestyle. As far as they're concerned, enough is enough. This is a family who has their priorities straight. Anyway, I believe God purposely sent these two families to visit me so my message would be crystal clear: It IS possible to live on the plantation without becoming enslaved. Just because Donna Partow can't do it doesn't mean no one can.

My advice: Get together with your spouse, get on your knees before God, and ask him to show you whether or not a change is in order. 'Nuf said!!!

Reflections Along the Journey

1. In what way or ways have you been enslaved by the status quo?

2. What are some practical ways you can begin living in freedom, even in your current circumstances?

3. Is it possible that you need to leave the plantation in order to enter into your freedom? This is a huge step! Make a list of the pros and cons of making a move to a place where you can live a simpler life.

4. Write out a prayer asking God's guidance concerning any changes you may need to make.

5. What key lesson did you glean from today's study?

Freedom Truths:

- Don't allow the status quo to enslave you.
- Some former slaves can remain on the plantation and live in freedom. But some have to leave the plantation before they can enter into freedom.

Day Four

Sold Into Slavery

You intended to harm me, but God intended it for good to accomplish what is now being done, the saving of many lives.
Genesis 50:20

Sometimes we sell ourselves into slavery. Sometimes we are sold into slavery by someone we love, someone who is supposed to love us. Read the following account from the life of Joseph and note how he became a slave:

So Joseph went after his brothers and found them near Dothan. But they saw him in the distance, and before he reached them, they plotted to kill him.

"Here comes that dreamer!" they said to each other. "Come now, let's kill him and throw him into one of these cisterns and say that a ferocious animal devoured him. Then we'll see what comes of his dreams."

When Reuben heard this, he tried to rescue him from their hands. "Let's not take his life," he said. "Don't shed any blood. Throw him into this cistern here in the desert, but don't lay a hand on him." Reuben said this to rescue him from them and take him back to his father.

So when Joseph came to his brothers, they stripped him of his robe—the richly ornamented robe he was wearing—and they took him and threw him into the cistern. Now the cistern was empty; there was no water in it.

As they sat down to eat their meal, they looked up and saw a caravan of Ishmaelites coming from Gilead. Their camels were loaded with spices, balm and myrrh, and they were on their way to take them down to Egypt.

Judah said to his brothers, "What will we gain if we kill our brother and cover up his blood? Come, let's sell him to the Ishmaelites and not lay our hands on him; after all, he is our brother, our own flesh and blood." His brothers agreed.

So when the Midianite merchants came by, his brothers pulled Joseph up out of the cistern and sold him for twenty shekels of silver to the Ishmaelites, who took him to Egypt. (Genesis 37: 17b–28)

For twenty shekels of silver, Joseph was sold into slavery against his will. He was destined to suffer hardship, not through his own choices but through the choices of others. Joseph couldn't change his circumstances, but he could choose his attitude. He couldn't control other people's actions, but he could choose his own reactions. Most of you are familiar with his story: how he conducted himself so honorably and with such wisdom that even though a slave he became ruler of all Egypt. (If you don't know the story, you can read it in Genesis 37–50.)

Eventually God allowed Joseph to see the purpose for his slavery: "You intended to harm me, but God intended it for good to accomplish what is now being done, the saving of many lives," he says to his brothers.

Perhaps you, too, have become enslaved, not by your own choice but through the choices of others. Perhaps your husband or your children or some other significant person in your life has made decisions that have left you feeling enslaved. We'll talk more about the emotional impact of suffering from other people's choices in Week 7, "Emancipate Your Fellow Slaves, Part Two." For now I want us to come face-to-face with the practical realities.

I'm saddened by the number of young mothers who feel they have to work outside the home. In some cases, the real culprit is their enslavement to status or the status quo, as we've already seen. I've had women who live in $200,000 homes tell me straight-faced that they "had" to work. Basically they were telling me that maintaining their house and their lifestyle was more important than their children's well-being. I call that slavery, pure and simple.

However, I am meeting an increasing number of women whose husbands *insist* that they work. Even if the woman is willing to lower the family's standard of living in order to stay at home, the husband is not. So she's enslaved by his foolish priorities. I also meet women whose husbands simply don't earn enough income to maintain even a modest standard of living. Granted, in some cases the guy is just a bum who refuses to get a real job. But in other cases, he lacks the qualifications to succeed. I'm thinking now of a woman I know who lives in a trailer park. Her husband works as hard as he can yet earns only minimum wage. This woman would love nothing more than to be at home with her children. Many times I've sat with her as she cried out to God for answers. It would certainly seem that God is in favor of a mom staying at home with her children, yet in this case it's simply not possible.

I also meet an appalling number of women who have been abandoned by their husbands. A friend of mine was deserted by her husband shortly after she gave birth to twins. She's doing everything she can just to survive, while her husband lives it up in a glamorous foreign country. Like many single moms, she has been reduced to virtual slavery, working day and night and living in a perpetual state of exhaustion.

Then there's my friend Debbie, one of the most godly women I've ever been privileged to know. She is an amazing mom who maintains a warm, wonderful home. Her husband is a deacon in the local church, which they've faithfully attended for fifteen years. Each morning this homeschooling mom leads her children in a time of Bible study. In the evening her husband leads family devotions. Then, as he tucks each child into bed, he prays a blessing over him. I'm telling you, this family is the salt of the earth. They're not a bunch of phonies. (I have a finely tuned phony-detection device, so believe me, I know a phony when I meet one.) They are a wonderful, godly family.

That's why I'll never forget the night their twenty-two-year-old son was featured on the local news *for shooting a police officer*. He is currently serving a twenty-year sentence in a federal prison. Once a month the family piles into their minivan to pay him a visit.

Was Debbie a bad mom? No, she was a fabulous mom. Is she suffering for her own mistakes? No, her son made his own choices. Unfortunately those choices had a heartbreaking effect on everyone who loved him. He will be in chains for many years to come. In a real sense, so will his family.

I wish I could say Debbie has discovered some grand purpose in all this suffering. So far she hasn't. But God isn't finished yet. Someday Debbie may be able to say along with Joseph, "You intended to harm me, but God intended it for good to accomplish what is now being done, the saving of many lives." Already God has given her greater sensitivity to families in crisis.

You may recall that God's children made some stupid choices too. Adam and Eve chose to eat of the forbidden fruit, and their family has been suffering ever since. The process of getting their family back on track took thousands of years and required the death of our Lord, but God was able to deliver the human family from bondage.

I'm not sure how comforting this thought is for you, but perhaps you need a bigger picture. Perhaps God is doing something in your life that will liberate *future generations* of your family. Although you are reaping consequences from past choices, as you make better choices for the future, your children and grandchildren, even your great-grandchildren, will surely benefit.

Reflections Along the Journey

1. Do you feel enslaved as a result of someone else's choices? Describe.

2. What possible lessons might God want you to learn through your current situation?

3. Is it possible that what others intended for evil God intended for good? How so?

4. Write out a prayer asking God to show you how the things you are suffering may accomplish good.

5. What key lesson did you glean from today's study?

Freedom Truths:

- Sometimes we are enslaved not by our own choices but by the choices of those we love.
- God may be doing a work in your life designed to benefit future generations.

Day Five

Enslaved by Another's Choices

O ne of the most difficult things to do is to forgive someone who has harmed you. Their choice—their abuse—can leave physical, emotional,and even spiritual scars.

Author Marsha Crockett's recent book, *Sanctuary*,[1] is filled with stories about women who found in God a safe place, a gentle touch, when life dealt the unexpected. One person Marsha introduces us to is Laurel, who was enslaved by another's choices but found deliverance through God's unfailing love, which led her to relinquish her captors into his hands.

Growing up, Laurel's family looked like a typical family. She would walk to school with her older sister and younger brother and even wave to neighbors on the way down the street. But deep down, she wondered, *Did anyone hear? Did they hear my daddy threatening to kill us last night because of the bad grade I made at school?*

Beyond the unpredictable and raging threats of death, Laurel's father was also a con artist. If it wasn't police officers or the FBI knocking at their door, it was someone Dad had swindled. He hid guns all over the house because of the dozens of break-ins that occurred. Many nights the sound of a cocking gun or someone trying to break through the front door woke Laurel.

During her childhood, Laurel's father was in and out of prison. As a result of his long absences, the family often lived in poverty, with no running water or electricity for weeks at a time. Laurel's mom dealt with life through denial and control. She always pretended they were a normal, happy family and that she was an ordinary housewife like all the other women on the block and at church. Laurel's mom had started taking her children to church when they were quite young.

---

[1]Adapted from Marsha Crockett, *Sanctuary: Finding Safe Places for a Woman's Soul* (Minneapolis, Minn.: Bethany House Publishers, 1999), 117–21.

Laurel immediately fell in love with Jesus. Still, as she grew older, she continued to wonder if anyone knew or cared about her suffering. She thought life would be better if she tried to "be good." But when that failed to stop the abuse, she rebelled and became full of raging anger. Laurel felt ugly, dirty, unworthy.

Laurel's chaotic life continued after she was out on her own. She lived a promiscuous life for years, trying to cover the hurt. With each failure, though, God's mercy continued to work in Laurel and to bring her to a point of obedience and submission to his leading. His grace created a yearning in her to forgive her offenders, which he ultimately used in her healing.

Over time, Laurel has tried to reach out to her parents. After years of no contact with her father, she had a brief encounter with him in which he made it clear he wanted no part in mending past hurts. Her mother has turned her back on the church and on God, believing instead that she can create happiness on her own. Laurel prays for her mother and father even as she continues the process of learning to forgive.

Only God can change hearts. What a beautiful moment, when the captive, having entered into her own freedom, in turn reaches out to her captors. It is even as Joseph said to his brothers: "You intended to harm me, but God intended it for good."

Reflections Along the Journey

1. How was God able to take that which was intended to harm Joseph and transform it into something good?

2. Can you think of a situation in your life where someone intended to harm you, but God transformed it into something good?

3. Can you think of a situation you are facing *right now* where someone is harming you intentionally?

4. What are some ways in which God might transform your situation into something good in the future?

5. Write out a prayer expressing forgiveness toward one who has hurt you.

6. What key lesson did you glean from today's study?

7. Write out this week's verse from memory:

Freedom Truths:

- Nothing is more beautiful than when a former captive, having entered into his own freedom, sets his captors free.
- When people intend harm, God may intend the same for good.

Weekly Review:

See if you can fill in the seven steps toward living in absolute freedom. Look in the back of the book if you need help.

F _____ your bondage

R _____ your Deliverer

E _____ your liberty

E _____ your fellow slaves

D _____ yourself in God

O _____ pockets of resistance

M _____ forward in absolute freedom

WEEK FOUR:
Receive Your Deliverer

This Week's Verse:

This is what the Lord says to you: "Do not be afraid or discouraged because of this vast army. For the battle is not yours, but God's. . . . You will not have to fight this battle. Take up your positions; stand firm and see the deliverance the Lord will give you."

2 Chronicles 20:15, 17 (selected portions)

Day One

Our Deliverer Is Coming

He was sent to be their ruler and deliverer by God himself. . . .
This is that Moses who told the Israelites, "God will send you a
prophet like me from your own people."

Acts 7:35, 37

Throughout virtually all of their history, the Israelites have rallied
one another with the cry, "Our deliverer is coming!" When they lived
in bondage under the Egyptians for four hundred years, it was the
hope of a deliverer that sustained them. At last God fulfilled his promise in the person of Moses. Today we'll read an extended passage from
God's Word concerning the first deliverer:

When Moses was forty years old, he decided to visit his fellow Israelites. He saw one of them being mistreated by an Egyptian, so he went to his defense and avenged him by killing the
Egyptian. Moses thought that his own people would realize that
God was using him to rescue them, but they did not. The next
day Moses came upon two Israelites who were fighting. He tried
to reconcile them by saying, "Men, you are brothers; why do you
want to hurt each other?"

But the man who was mistreating the other pushed Moses
aside and said, "Who made you ruler and judge over us? Do you
want to kill me as you killed the Egyptian yesterday?" When
Moses heard this, he fled to Midian, where he settled as a for-
eigner and had two sons.

After forty years had passed, an angel appeared to Moses in
the flames of a burning bush in the desert near Mount Sinai.
When he saw this, he was amazed at the sight. As he went over
to look more closely, he heard the Lord's voice: "I am the God of
your fathers, the God of Abraham, Isaac and Jacob." Moses trem-

bled with fear and did not dare to look.

Then the Lord said to him, "Take off your sandals; the place where you are standing is holy ground. I have indeed seen the oppression of my people in Egypt. I have heard their groaning and have come down to set them free. Now come, I will send you back to Egypt."

This is the same Moses whom they had rejected with the words, "Who made you ruler and judge?" He was sent to be their ruler and deliverer by God himself, through the angel who appeared to him in the bush. He led them out of Egypt and did wonders and miraculous signs in Egypt, at the Red Sea and for forty years in the desert.

This is that Moses who told the Israelites, "God will send you a prophet like me from your own people." He was in the assembly in the desert, with the angel who spoke to him on Mount Sinai, and with our fathers; and he received living words to pass on to us.

But our fathers refused to obey him. Instead, they rejected him and in their hearts turned back to Egypt. (Acts 7:23–39)

Now read through the passage again and note anything that strikes you as relevant to our topic, living in absolute freedom. Answer the questions I've posed, but do not limit yourself to them. If you would like to gain additional insight, turn to Exodus 3.

1. Who was the deliverer?
2. Who sent the deliverer?
3. Why was the deliverer sent?
4. Having been set free, did the people live in freedom?

Reflections Along the Journey

1. Recap the key truths you gathered about the first deliverer.

2. What key lesson did you glean from today's study?

Freedom Truths:

- Throughout history the Israelites have rallied to the cry: "Our deliverer is coming!"
- Even after their deliverer led them to freedom, their hearts turned back to slavery.

Day Two

Our Deliverer Has Come

For he has rescued us from the dominion of darkness and brought us into the kingdom of the Son he loves, in whom we have redemption, the forgiveness of sins.

Colossians 1:13–14

Today I want to make some observations about the first deliverer, Moses, then explore similarities to the second Deliverer, Jesus. By extension, we'll take a look at the Israelites, who rarely got it right, and ourselves, in the hope that we *will* get it right!

First, the deliverer walked away from a kingdom and chose to live among an oppressed people. Indeed, Moses is commended in the Great Hall of Faith because "when he had grown up, he refused to be known as the son of Pharaoh's daughter. He chose to be mistreated along with the people of God rather than to enjoy the pleasures of sin for a short time" (Hebrews 11:24–25).

Second, it was God who had sent the deliverer. He did not come on his own; he came with a mission from God. God said to Moses, "So now, go. I am sending you to Pharaoh to bring my people the Israelites out of Egypt" (Exodus 3:10).

Third, the deliverer was sent because of God's great love and mercy. "The Lord said, 'I have indeed seen the misery of my people in Egypt. I have heard them crying out because of their slave drivers, and I am concerned about their suffering. So I have come down to rescue them from the hand of the Egyptians and to bring them up out of that land into [the Promised Land]' " (Exodus 3:7–8a).

Fourth, having witnessed the mighty miracles that brought about their deliverance, and having been set free, the people failed to *enter into* their freedom. "In their hearts [they] turned back to Egypt."

That's why they wandered around in the desert for another forty years. And even after entering into the Promised Land, their hearts continually harkened back to the false gods of Egypt.

Getting the people out of Egypt was one thing; getting Egypt out of the people was quite another.

Already you can see the parallels to Christ, our Deliverer. First, he left his throne in heaven to dwell among a people who were in bondage (John 1:14; Isaiah 40:3–5).

Second, he did not come on his own; he was sent by the Father, as the Scripture bears out, again and again: "For the very work that the Father has given me to finish, and which I am doing, testifies that the Father has sent me. And the Father who sent me has himself testified concerning me" (John 5:36–37).

"I stand with the Father, who sent me" (John 8:14b).

"For I did not speak of my own accord, but the Father who sent me commanded me what to say and how to say it" (John 12:49).

Third, he was sent because of God's great love and mercy for us: "For God so loved the world that he gave his one and only Son, that whoever believes in him shall not perish but have eternal life. For God did not send his Son into the world to condemn the world, but to save the world through him" (John 3:16–17).

Through the work of Christ, we were taken out of the land of slavery and brought into the promised land of freedom in Christ, for God "hath delivered us from the power of darkness, and hath translated us into the kingdom of his dear Son: In whom we have redemption through his blood, even the forgiveness of sins" (Colossians 1: 13–14 KJV).

God has delivered us from the power of darkness; we are no longer slaves of sin. However, now we come to the fourth and most unfortunate parallel: like the Israelites, many of us, having once been set free, have "turned back to Egypt in our hearts." We have failed to *enter into* our freedom.

Let us not live like the vast number of Israelites today who still await a Deliverer, who has already come. Our Deliverer has come. Enter into the freedom he offers.

Reflections Along the Journey

1. What are some of the parallels between Moses, the first deliverer, and Christ, our Deliverer?

2. What does it mean when we say that the people "turned back to Egypt in their hearts"?

3. In what way have you "turned back to Egypt" in your heart?

4. Write out a prayer of repentence for those times when you have "turned back to Egypt" in your heart.

5. What key lesson did you glean from today's study?

Freedom Truths:

- Let us not live like the Israelites, who still await a Deliverer who has already come.
- Our Deliverer has come. Enter into the freedom he offers.

Day Three

Who Will Deliver Me?

O wretched man that I am! who shall deliver me from the body
of this death? I thank God through Jesus Christ our Lord.

Romans 7:24–25 (KJV)

At first glance, it may seem ironic that the apostle Paul, who clearly knew and understood that the Deliverer had come, still cries out, "Who shall deliver ME?" Yet doesn't our own heart echo the cry? For the first three weeks of our study, we have faced our own bondage. And we must acknowledge that even as Christians who recognize the Deliverer, we still need deliverance in many areas of our lives. As we have seen the truth of our own depravity (a term no one uses anymore), we may have cried out, *What a wretched person I am! Who will deliver ME from this body of death?*

We know the theological answer: Christ is our deliverer. But this is not a cry of the head; it's a cry of the *heart*. It's almost as if God has cut down the barbed wire around the prison and declared us free— but we can't figure out how to get out of our cell.

Not long ago my daughter challenged me to a game of Monopoly. The only thing worse than paying rent and taxes is landing in jail. Guess who kept landing on "Go to Jail"? Yep, poor old mom. Eventually I became filled with dread whenever my silver shoe approached "Go to Jail" on the board. Then something magical happened: I acquired one of the coveted "Get Out of Jail Free" cards. Suddenly that prison cell had no power over me. The fear was gone! I knew *in advance* that I had a way of escape.

Do you know what I think we need to carry in our possession at all times? A "Get Out of Jail Free" card.

So, here's how it works. You carry this card everywhere you go. Then, when you're "playing the game of life" and suddenly find yourself locked in a prison cell, you take out the card and declare, "I don't have to stay here one minute longer! I've been set free." Even better, when you sense danger up ahead—an area that usually sends you straight into bondage—take out your card with confidence, knowing you don't have to spend one millisecond in that prison. You have your freedom guaranteed in advance.

I'm not kidding! Try this. Make several photocopies of this card or design your own on index cards.[1] On the back, you might write any of the following verses (or others that come to mind):

"The Lord is my rock, and my fortress, and my deliverer" (2 Samuel 22:2 KJV).

"The Lord is my rock, and my fortress, and my deliverer; my God, my strength, in whom I will trust; my buckler, and the horn of my salvation, and my high tower. I will call upon the Lord, who is worthy to be praised: so shall I be saved from mine enemies" (Psalm 18:2–3 KJV).

God is "my fortress; my high tower, and my deliverer; my shield, and he in whom I trust" (Psalm 144:2 KJV).

Notice how all of these verses about our deliverer paint vivid pictures of God as the place we can run to for safety. If you found yourself in the midst of a flood, you would *run* to a rock. In the midst of a battle, you would *run* to a fortress. When your enemies threatened to destroy you, you would *run* to a high tower.

It is interesting to note that in all of these word pictures, we are the ones who need to do the running. The rock, the fortress, the high tower—none of these run to us. They stand unmoved and unmovable. They are always the same. They are there ready to protect us, ready

---

[1]You'll find a "Get Out of Jail Free" card in the back of the book, along with your Scripture memory cards.

to deliver us from harm, but it's up to us to run to them.

Our Deliverer *has come*; he is standing by waiting to deliver us from harm. Why would we *not* run to him?

Who will deliver you? God will. Run to him.

Reflections Along the Journey

1. Have you ever heard yourself crying out, "Oh, wretched man that I am! Who will deliver me from this body of death?" Describe those moments.

2. If you are truly brave, describe what "besetting sin" sends you to the place of crying out for deliverance.

3. How might the "Get Out of Jail Free" card make a difference when you find yourself in bondage—or heading toward it?

4. Write out a prayer expressing your heart's cry for deliverance.

5. What key lesson did you glean from today's study?

Freedom Truths:

- God has given you the opportunity to "Get Out of Jail Free."
- Your Deliverer has come; run to him.

Day Four

God, My Champion

O Lord, you have seen this; be not silent.
Do not be far from me, O Lord.
Awake, and rise to my defense!
Contend for me, my God and Lord.
Vindicate me in your righteousness,
O Lord my God.

Psalm 35:22–24

Back in the days of knights in shining armor, if two people had a conflict, they would resort to battle. The opponents would joust until one either capitulated or dropped dead.

Sounds a lot like marriages today, doesn't it?

Just kidding!

Eventually a system evolved where the wealthy would hire someone to fight the battle on his behalf. That person was called a "champion." So when a conflict arose, rather than engaging in battle, the one fortunate enough to have a champion on the payroll would send someone else to fight on his behalf.

I'd like to suggest that what many of us need is a "champion." Fortunately, we don't have to pay any extra money for the service. We already have a Champion. But we've been so busy fighting our own battles that we haven't noticed him standing by, ready to fight on our behalf.

I meet many wives who need a champion in their own home. Ideally, our husbands should champion our cause, but a husband who champions his wife is a rarity these days. When the children cry out against Mom's "injustice," and Dad pleads *their* case rather than Mom's, she needs a champion. When there's a conflict with a neigh-

91

bor, and your husband heaps additional burning coals upon your head rather than defending your cause, you need a champion.

When your husband comes home and asks, "What did you do all day?" and the details are a blur in your mind—the only thing you remember for sure is that you didn't sit down all day—you need a champion.

Unfortunately, we're tempted to be our own champion. We are not equal to such battles; we need to rely on our Champion, the Lord Jesus:

> This is what the Lord says to you, "Do not be afraid or discouraged because of this vast army. For the battle is not yours, but God's. . . . You will not have to fight this battle. Take up your positions; stand firm and see the deliverance the Lord will give you" (2 Chronicles 20:15b, 17).

Did you get that? We should not live in fear or discouragement in our own homes. Fear may not be a big problem for most Christian women, but discouragement is epidemic. We need to realize that the battle for our homes is not our battle to fight. Yes, we need to take up our positions. We need to be in our homes diligently doing what we're supposed to be doing. Yes, we need to stand firm rather than run away when the going gets tough. But we don't have to fight. We don't have to champion our own cause in the eyes of our husbands or our children. Let God do that, because "the battle is the Lord's" (1 Samuel 17:47b).

As far as I'm concerned, one of the most comforting names of God in the Bible is *El Roi*, which means "the God who sees." You may remember Amy Grant's rendition of "El Shaddai" (music and lyrics by Michael Card), in which she sings, "To the outcast on her knees, you were the God who really sees." The song is referring to Hagar, who had been wrongly treated by her husband-of-sorts, Abraham. Basically he had used her and cast her aside (see Genesis 16, 21). She had no one to defend her against such injustice, but she cried out to *El Roi*, to the God who sees, and he came to her rescue.

Do you feel your husband—or someone else—has treated you unjustly? Call out to the God who not only sees but who also will come to your rescue. Make Psalm 35 your prayer:

O Lord, you have seen this; be not silent.
Do not be far from me, O Lord.
Awake, and rise to my defense!
Contend for me, my God and Lord.
Vindicate me in your righteousness,
O Lord my God. (vv. 22–24)

Reflections Along the Journey

1. Do you need a champion? On what battlefield?

2. How could relying on your Champion—rather than fighting the battle yourself—make a difference in your homelife?

3. Do you find comfort in the name *El Roi*? Explain why.

4. Write out a prayer of Thanksgiving to El Roi.

5. What key lesson did you glean from today's study?

Freedom Truths:

- God is our Champion.
- We do not need to fight our own battles; we need only stand firm and see the Lord's deliverance.

Day Five

From the River to the Sea

The words on the page shocked us. We couldn't believe what we were reading.

My daughter Nichole had agreed to share her testimony with a magazine under two conditions: first, that they give the glory to God, and second, that they resist the temptation to trash her family of origin. You see, Nichole came to live with us when she was twelve years old. She had been left homeless when both her mom and dad were sent to prison. While running from the police and the Child Protective Services, Nichole had lived in some fifty different places, including *cars*. When she came into our home, she was a four-week-old Christian with a duffel bag containing her few worldly possessions— and a lifetime of emotional baggage.

But God began to do a mighty work in her life. He infused her with a sense of purpose. He called her into ministry and poured out every spiritual blessing upon her. His anointing upon her life was so powerful that total strangers would remark, "I don't know what it is, but there's just something about her. A glow, a radiance." Of course, it was the Spirit of God they were sensing.

God enabled her to travel to Africa, England, and Mexico on mission trips and to travel around the country sharing her testimony with thousands of teenagers. In the process, he used her to bring 148 teenagers to a knowledge of himself.[2]

Through a variety of circumstances, God orchestrated an interview with this magazine. It was nothing we had done, nothing we had sought. Needless to say, Nichole was ecstatic. The little girl who did not have a *single picture* from the first twelve years of her life was told she would be featured on the *cover* of a magazine. This was God's

---

[2]I've told Nichole's story in greater detail in my previous book, *Walking in Total God-Confidence*.

doing, and it was marvelous in our eyes.

Over and over again throughout the interview, Nichole pointed to the present—what God was doing in and through her, and to the future—what she believed God was calling her to do and the message she wanted to bring to her generation.

But the article so dishonored her parents that we called to propose changes. Changes that would point *away* from her earthly parents and toward her heavenly Father. Changes that would point away from the past and toward the future. I was told point-blank that either the article would run *precisely* as they had written it or it would not run at all. The magazine's editor instructed me that we had exactly five minutes to make our decision. I said we would need to pray about it. Although, come to think of it, what were we going to pray? "Dear God, should Nichole dishonor her parents even though your Word says, 'Honor your father and mother'?" It was really a no-brainer, but I knew it had to be Nichole's decision, not mine. I also knew this cover story meant the world to her. I just wasn't sure what she would be willing to sacrifice to get something she so desperately wanted.

I hung up the phone and looked at Nichole. We were both crying. I finally blurted out: "It's your call, pumpkin." She shook her head with finality. "I can't do it," she said.

I've never been more proud of anyone in my life.

Over the next several weeks we agonized over what had happened. The hardest thing for Nichole was the realization that God had orchestrated all of this. It was as if he *set her up* for heartbreak. She could forgive the magazine's staff, because she knew they had good intentions. They just didn't fully understand the complexity of her situation. She was struggling to forgive God. She asked over and over again, "Why would God hand me something and then take it away at the last minute?"

Finally, I said to her: "I don't claim to understand everything that's happened. But I do know one thing: God didn't pull you from the river to drown you in the sea."[3]

She already knew the slogan by heart. I had reminded her of that truth over and over again. It has become a Partow family maxim.

Do you realize the truth of those words? Do you realize that God

---

[3]I'm indebted to Russ Taff for this phrase.

didn't pull you from the river to drown you in the sea? He didn't deliver you from the kingdom of darkness; he didn't deliver you from whatever bondages you were in; he didn't bring you this far—to destroy you.

You know it in your heart, don't you? You know it makes sense, it rings true. *God didn't pull you from the river to drown you in the sea.* He pulled you from the river because he has something in mind for your life. If he didn't, he wouldn't have delivered you from the rapids in the first place.

Reflections Along the Journey

1. What river did God pull *you* from?

2. Have you ever felt like God pulled you from the river just to drown you in the sea? Describe the circumstance.

3. If the situation has been resolved, how did God deliver you?

4. If you are in the midst of the situation, what reassurance do you find in today's lesson?

5. Write out a prayer thanking God for "pulling you from the river."

6. What key lesson did you glean from today's study?

7. Write out this week's verse from memory:

Freedom Truths:

- God didn't pull you from the river to drown you in the sea.
- God has a purpose in mind for you; otherwise he wouldn't have delivered you in the first place.

Weekly Review:

See if you can fill in the seven steps toward living in absolute freedom. Look in the back of the book if you need help.

F _____ your bondage

R _____ your Deliverer

E _____ your liberty

E _____ your fellow slaves

D _____ yourself in God

O _____ pockets of resistance

M _____ forward in absolute freedom

WEEK FIVE:
Embrace Your Liberty

This Week's Verse:

Jesus replied, "I tell you the truth, everyone who sins is a slave
to sin. Now a slave has no permanent place in the family, but
a son belongs to it forever. So if the Son sets you free,
you will be free indeed."

John 8:34–36

Day One

Liberating Your Heart

There is no fear in love; but perfect love casteth out fear: because fear hath torment. He that feareth is not made perfect in love.

1 John 4:18 (KJV)

In 1976 a seventeen-year-old Iranian named Kamran boarded a Boeing 747 headed for New York City. This flight was not the fulfillment of a dream but rather the end result of years spent ditching school to pursue his passion for rock-and-roll music. Having failed in school, he was going to America for one reason: to prove he could succeed, and then get back to Iran as soon as possible.

As he flew toward the unknown, he was only certain of one thing: he would never marry an American woman. He knew all about them. After all, he'd seen every episode of *Dallas* and *Dynasty*. Worse than what he'd seen was what he heard, over and over again: *"If you marry an American woman, she will surely abandon you. Don't turn your back; don't trust her for a minute."*

Two years later the Iranian Revolution broke out and Kamran's whole world was turned upside down. His parents couldn't leave the country, and he couldn't get back in. Suddenly he found himself isolated in a foreign land with no hope for the future. He didn't know if he would ever see his family again.

Into this chaos of heartache walked an unsuspecting newborn believer in Christ.

Me.

From Kamran's point of view, it was love at first sight, and he was determined to make me his own. He instantly gave part of his heart to me. Unfortunately, the rest of his heart remained in bondage to

100

fear. He was so afraid of losing yet another person he loved that he held onto me with a deathlike grip.

Proverbs 31:11 says, "The heart of her husband doth safely trust in her" (KJV), yet no matter how hard I tried to earn my husband's trust, it was impossible. Since he was afraid of losing me, he determined to make me equally afraid of leaving him. He succeeded until November 1996. Then, in the midst of a family crisis, his worst fear was realized: I walked out the door and didn't come back that night. It was the bravest thing I'd ever done.

My husband had always threatened that he would kill me if I tried to leave him. I never knew if he was bluffing but had always been too frightened to try to find out. And I let that fear control me for seventeen years. Now here I was spending the night sleeping on a couch at a friend's house. Somewhere in the middle of that night, there came a loud banging on the door. I woke up terrified but slowly approached the door.

So this is it, I thought. *This is the end for me.*

The banging became more persistent as I struggled with the lock. My mind raced: *I'm opening this door so he can kill me!* Finally the lock gave way, and the door swung open.

It was my girlfriend's husband. He was as shocked to see me as I was relieved to see him. He was returning from an overseas trip and was upset because he had given specific instructions to his wife not to lock the door.

It's been said that the best way to conquer a fear is to open the door and let it in. That's what I did. The next morning I opened the door again, and on the other side, rather than the big bad Iranian man I expected to see, I saw a frightened, trembling little boy. I saw a man whose heart was in bondage to fear.

I determined that I would not live one more moment of my life in bondage to fear. Not my fears, not his fears. I took as my new motto, Fear God Only, and began trying to walk in obedience to all that God had called me to be and to do. It had been seventeen long years since God first laid on my heart a vision for a speaking ministry. Now I found the courage to step out in faith. Since then, God has taken me all over the country, speaking in churches large and small. Farm churches in the Midwest; urban churches along the East Coast. I have spoken to countless denominations: Assemblies of God, Baptist,

Catholic. You name it! Today my heart soars as I consider all that God is doing in and through my life, but it never could have happened as long as I lived in bondage to fear.

Is there someone or something you're clinging to out of fear? If so, your heart is in bondage. Is there someone you hold captive to a jealous, possessive love? If so, your heart is in bondage. Is there someone you think you need *more than you need God*? If so, your heart is in bondage.

Perhaps you are being controlled by someone who clings to you out of fear. Perhaps someone in your life has a heart in bondage to fear and you have allowed his/her bondage to become your bondage. That's no way to live, my friend. Believe me, I know. Fear God only. Then allow God's perfect love to cast out all other fear and liberate your heart.

Reflections Along the Journey

1. Is there someone or something you are clinging to out of fear? How is fear affecting your relationship?

2. Is there someone you think you need more than God? How is that false perspective affecting your relationship with that person?

3. Are you now or have you ever been in a relationship controlled by fear? What is/was it like?

4. Write out a prayer inviting God's perfect love to cast out all fear from your heart.

5. What key lesson did you glean from today's study?

Freedom Truths:

- If you are clinging to someone or something out of fear, your heart is in bondage.
- If there is someone you think you need more than God, your heart is in bondage.

Day Two

Liberating Your Mind, Part One

Do not conform any longer to the pattern of this world, but be transformed by the renewing of your mind.

Romans 12:2

The worst thing about being a Christian author is that God makes you live it before he lets you write it. For the past eleven days I haven't been able to write a single sentence. Why? Because my mind absolutely refuses to focus on that which is pure and holy. I'm sitting in my office, late on a Friday night. There's a violent thunderstorm raging outside, like the storm that's been raging in my mind.

I've been allowing the "what ifs?" to consume me. I've been thinking about getting older. I've been looking in the mirror and noticing that whatever I once had going *for me* is rapidly going *from me*. I'm realizing that I've already made most of the big life-altering decisions, so the path ahead of me promises few opportunities to radically change course.

I hear myself mumbling, "So this is it. This is my life." And I even occasionally hear the old tune floating through my head, posing the question all of us dread most: *"Is that all there is?"*

So my mind has turned itself to imagining alternative scenarios, different choices, different paths. And I've been following those thoughts through the dark recesses of my mind, like a child whose curiosity gets the better of him and he ends up lost in the forest—*with nightfall closing in.* Sometimes my mind travels into the past, picking up remnants of memories to build upon. Sometimes it builds on the material around me. Always it beckons: Follow me a step further—just one step further.

And so I've been indulging thoughts I know I should flee. *Just one step further*, I promise myself, *then I'll turn back. I'll find my way out again.* Instead, I keep going further and further, deeper and deeper, until everything is so murky, so shadowy, I want to crawl under the covers, close my eyes, and make it all go away. . . . Maybe it's all those Reese's Pieces I've been pigging out on lately.

Into this darkness, I hear God calling me . . . out of the darkness, into his blessed light.[1]

I'm thinking back now to a Christian seminar I attended last Saturday. The speaker kept quoting a portion of Colossians 1:27: "Christ in you . . ." I finally wanted to jump out of my chair to finish the phrase: ". . . the hope of glory."

"Christ in you, the hope of glory."

The hope of glory.

That's what we must cling to. The realization that this is *not* it, that this is *not* all there is. There's another side, another place, with him in glory. There my mind will overflow with all that is good and pure and holy and beautiful. There all my choices will be right. There will be no darkness, no murkiness, nothing gray. There no storms will rage; my mind will be at peace.

For now I must mount my courage and wage the battle. God has given me a command: "Do not conform any longer to the pattern of this world, but be transformed by the renewing of your mind."

Don't conform. Be transformed. Renew your mind.

These are things I must choose to do, every day. No one can choose them for me. No one can crawl into my mind and hold up a Stop sign. Only I have the power to do that.

Have you ever let your mind become enslaved to "what ifs?" Have you ever felt like a captive, being led deeper and deeper toward thoughts you know you should flee but feel powerless to escape? You *can* escape. You have the power to liberate your mind: "Christ in you, the hope of glory." No "what ifs?" can possibly compare to the certainty of dwelling forever with him.

Think about that.

Reflections Along the Journey

1. Have you ever let your mind become enslaved to "what ifs?" How did it affect you mentally and emotionally?

---

[1]A phrase borrowed from a Lynne Paasch song. Thanks, Lynne, for your ministry of music.

2. How can "Christ in you, the hope of glory" set you free from the "what ifs?"

3. What are some specific ways you can obey God's commands: Don't conform? Be transformed? Renew your mind?

4. Write out a prayer repenting of "what ifs?"

5. What key lesson did you glean from today's study?

Freedom Truths:

- Our mind can become enslaved to "what ifs?"
- God has commanded us: Don't conform. Be transformed. Renew your mind.

Day Three

Liberating Your Mind, Part Two

For though we live in the world, we do not wage war as the world does. The weapons we fight with are not the weapons of the world. On the contrary, they have divine power to demolish strongholds. We demolish arguments and every pretension that sets itself up against the knowledge of God, and we take captive every thought to make it obedient to Christ.

2 Corinthians 10:3–5

Yesterday we talked about how our minds can become enslaved to "what ifs?" and I described how mental battles sometimes rage in our heads. The only way to liberate our minds is to "take captive every thought." Therefore, God's Word says it's up to us to wield the weapons of warfare. That means we have to jump into the battle. If we sit idly by, hoping the thought will flee or surrender, we're just deceiving ourselves. We have to *fight*. When destructive or unhealthy thoughts come, we must catch them in midair, face them squarely, and battle them biblically.

Entire books have been written on the business of demolishing strongholds and taking thoughts captive. Now that I've admitted how often I'm on the losing side of such battles, you're wise to mistrust my advice on how to secure victory. So let me point you elsewhere: *The Three Battlegrounds* by Francis Frangipane.[2]

He defines a stronghold as "a demonically induced pattern of thinking. . . . It is a house made of thoughts, which has become a dwelling place for satanic activity."[3]

---

[2]Francis Frangipane, *The Three Battlegrounds* (Cedar Rapids, Iowa: Advancing Church Publications, 1989).
[3]Frangipane has a different theological perspective than I do, so I don't agree with him on every point. Nevertheless, I found his book quite fascinating.

The visual image of a house of thoughts is powerful, isn't it? You enter into a brightly lit foyer, just stopping by for a brief visit. The next thing you know, you're sleeping on a cot down in the pitch-dark basement with no immediate plans of moving out.

From another perspective, a house is built one brick at a time. We do that, too, don't we? It starts with a Mel Gibson movie. Brick one. You turn on a soap opera in the afternoon. Brick two. You have some spare time; rather than reading the Word of God, you begin to day-dream. Brick three. Your husband emotionally hurts you, so you allow yourself to dream of the man on the white horse. Brick four. Fleeting thoughts begin to gather, forming a habitation—a place you can run to whenever real life disappoints you.

Of particular interest to me was Frangipane's assertion that "the energies we expend in keeping our sins secret are the actual 'materials' of which a stronghold is made."[4] If that's the case, I have certainly demolished a stronghold or two during these past two days.

So what's the solution? Shine the light of God's truth into the darkness. Read God's Word aloud. Tell yourself the truth. Name the lies you've been telling yourself. Play praise music. Sing along. Most of all, repent. Admit that the sins in your mind are *real sins*. Jesus obviously took sins of the mind very seriously: "But I tell you that anyone who looks at a woman lustfully has already committed adultery with her in his heart" (Matthew 5:28).

Of course, lust is just one way our minds can become enslaved. We can also become enslaved to jealousy, resentment, bitterness, anger—any sin we can *act* upon we can also *dwell* upon. For example, have you ever preached silent sermons? You know what I mean. Someone really ticks you off—at church, at work, in your neighborhood—and although you haven't said anything to them *verbally*, you've really given them "what for" in front of your bathroom mirror! What does God think of these silent sermons? Here's how Jesus put it: "You have heard that it was said to the people long ago, 'Do not murder, and anyone who murders will be subject to judgment.' But I tell you that anyone who is angry with his brother will be subject to judgment" (Matthew 5:21–22).

God is calling us both to forgive and to seek his forgiveness. We

---

[4]Frangipane, 18.

must begin taking mental sins seriously and stop deceiving ourselves: *Well, I'm not doing anything wrong. My little fantasies aren't hurting anyone.* They are hurting you, and, more significantly, they hurt your heavenly Father. That's because all sin is *against God*, against his rule and authority over our lives.

David wrote, after committing adultery with Bathsheba (and you can bet it began with a thought):

> For I know my transgressions,
> and my sin is always before me.
> Against you, you only, have I sinned
> and done what is evil in your sight,
> so that you are proved right when you speak
> and justified when you judge. (Psalm 51:3–4)

God in his sovereignty has allowed us to be exactly where we are. He wants us to live in our own homes, not in some imaginary house of thoughts. So take those thoughts captive, lock them up, and refuse to visit them, even during visiting hours.

Reflections Along the Journey

1. What does it mean to "take captive every thought"?

2. Have you been building a house of thoughts?

3. Are there thought patterns you need to repent of?

4. Write out a prayer repenting of wrong thought patterns.

5. What key lesson did you glean from today's study?

Freedom Truths:

- In order to liberate our minds, we must "take every thought captive."
- A stronghold is a "house of thoughts" where the enemy invites us to dwell.

Day Four

Liberating Your Spirit

> *God is spirit, and his worshipers must worship in spirit and in truth.*
>
> John 4:24

What does it mean to worship God in spirit? Does it mean we have to whip ourselves into an emotional frenzy? Do we have to have a particular set of feelings or some predefined spiritual "experience"? As is often the case, the church seems to be at two extremes: those who worship enthusiastically but seem to be less attentive to doctrinal truths, and those whose grasp of God's truth is rock solid but who unfortunately seem quite intimidated by what is called "spirit-filled worship."

Is there a balance? Of course there is! It's just that I'm going to reach back into the sixteenth century to uncover it. I am referring to the teaching of John of the Cross, born in Spain in 1542. He was a man who was tortured for his faith, a man who found absolute freedom in prison in the midst of unspeakable suffering. Living in bondage, he learned how to be free within. How? Through contemplating the love of God:

> Allow Him to infuse into your soul *His* breath of eternal life, *His* light of knowing, *His* fire of love. This is nothing like striving with your mind to understand Him, not at all like generating kind Christian acts out of a good and willing determination to obey Him. It is letting Him come in to the inner chambers of your soul and to show himself to you.[5]

This type of contemplation doesn't come easy to modern man; it

---

[5]John of the Cross, David Hazard, ed., *You Set My Spirit Free* (Minneapolis, Minn.: Bethany House Publishers, 1994), 98.

seems irrational. Moreover, when we try not to strive, we start striving not to strive. We know nothing of solitude, nothing of rest, nothing of being completely emptied of ourselves. Yet such difficulties are not entirely new. John of the Cross addresses them directly:

> You may be the kind who resists the idea of advancing in spiritual growth by means of *contemplation*—that is, by quieting your soul and by emptying yourself of lower concepts of God, so He can reveal himself to your spirit as He really is.

Let me ask you: Have you ever seriously tried contemplation? I know, I know, you're conjuring up a bunch of New Age gurus sitting cross-legged on a mountaintop awaiting the Harmonic Convergence. I've met some of these crystal-peddlers, so believe me, I understand your resistance. Nevertheless, don't let a perversion prevent you from entering into true worship.

Quieting your soul takes time. So make time. In a previous book, *Walking in Total God-Confidence*, I advocated silent retreats and have gotten wonderful feedback from many readers who said it was the most valuable lesson they learned. It's very simple: Go away for a weekend, ideally to a retreat center,[6] but a hotel will work, provided you're committed to *making it work*.

Incidentally, I think our Catholic brothers and sisters are way out in front of Protestants in this area. If you go to a Protestant conference or retreat center, they will have a jam-packed program (complete with mindless games) with every minute of the day scheduled. I've gotten to the point where I refuse to speak at a conference that will not allow times of *silence* and *contemplation* as part of the schedule. And I'm tempted to decline invitations to any event featuring games or fashion shows.

The Catholic tradition seems to be much more in tune with the importance of quiet contemplation. In fact, there are convents, monasteries, and retreat centers all over the country where you can go for a private, quiet retreat.

Several weeks prior to the retreat, begin to write down questions or issues that have been on your mind, questions you want God to

---

[6]Check out the new book by Timothy Jones, *A Place for God: A Guide to Spiritual Retreats and Retreat Centers* (New York: Doubleday), n.d. Included is an extensive directory of more than two hundred and fifty retreat centers in all fifty states and Canada.

answer. Write each question on a separate piece of paper and bring these with you. Also take with you: your Bible, a couple of pens, and an empty notebook. If you're an avid reader, you can take along a favorite Christian book, provided you promise not to read it the entire time. You might also consider *The Soul at Rest: A Journey into Contemplative Prayer* by Tricia Rhodes, and *Quiet Places: A Woman's Guide to Personal Retreat* by Jane Rubietta (both published by Bethany House).

After arriving at your destination, check in, but don't speak to anyone unless you absolutely have to. You can wear a nametag that simply states: "Silent Retreat." Or make small cards that explain your purpose. No TV. No radio. No phone. No music of any kind—not even Christian. And if you're truly brave: no clock. When I do a silent retreat, I follow the no-clock rule: I sleep when I'm tired and I wake up when God awakens me.

If you are accustomed to fasting, you may do so. Otherwise, I would encourage you to eat simple meals, especially fresh fruits and vegetables. Drink plenty of water. No junk food. If you can resist caffeine, so much the better. By doing these things, you are communicating to God: "Here I am, waiting on you. I am ready to hear anything and everything you have to say to me." In particular, you are open to answers to the questions you have written down.

You still your spirit within and you wait expectantly. As you read through God's Word, you are jotting down key verses. You are pondering their significance for your life. You are writing out your prayers. Then God begins to speak. Here's a beautifully descriptive excerpt from *You Set My Spirit Free*:

> Then God intervenes. He arranges things so that one day, all alone, there arises from within a sudden surprising awareness of the absolute emptiness of things. He may also bring not only emptiness but an overwhelming sense of isolation from others and of loss.
>
> How few see this bleak moment for what it is—a chance to see their need for something that is beyond themselves. For their mind will never be able to erase the horror of coming to the edge of this bottomless chasm, which is a look down into the deadness of our own soul apart from the life of God. If you have ever come to this precipice, you know how quickly the soul wants to flee

from itself and rush to find something—anything at all—to "fill" itself again with noise and activity.

This is the moment, however, when it can cross over—from its own empty silence into an expectant quiet that is alive with His presence, from anxious restlessness into a calming stillness. Suddenly the soul finds that within its dark chasm there is a secret well of water springing up to overflowing with light and eternal life.[7]

It is my prayer that through such times of quiet contemplation, God will truly liberate your spirit. Remember: "True worship must emerge now in the context of our daily lives, for no man will worship through the great battles of tomorrow who complains in the mere skirmishes of today."[8]

Reflections Along the Journey

1. What do you think it means to worship God in spirit?

2. What do you think of the idea of taking a silent retreat? If possible, begin now to make plans for a time alone with God.

3. What key lesson did you glean from today's study?

Freedom Truths:

- Times of silent contemplation can liberate our spirits.
- God is spirit and we must worship him in spirit and in truth.

---

[7]John of the Cross, 47.
[8]Frangipane, 69.

Day Five

Liberating Your Will

This day I call heaven and earth as witnesses against you that I have set before you life and death, blessings and curses. Now choose life, so that you and your children may live and that you may love the Lord your God, listen to his voice, and hold fast to him.
Deuteronomy 30:19–20

I once heard true freedom defined as "the power to do the things you know you ought to do, when and how you ought to do them." True freedom is the power to choose rightly, the power to live righteously, unhindered by sin. "God is said to be absolutely free because no one and nothing can hinder Him or compel Him or stop Him. He is able to do as he pleases always, everywhere, forever."[9] God alone can live in absolute freedom because sin has no power over him. He alone can always do what is right. However, to the degree that we imitate him, we will enjoy ever increasing levels of freedom so that no one and nothing can hinder us or stop us from glorifying God through our lives.

In order to enter into that freedom, we need to make right choices, choices that please God, day by day. Before we can liberate the will, we must first understand its function:

> The will has only one mode of action; its function is to choose, and with every choice we make we grow in force of character. . . . "Choose ye this day," is the command that comes to each of us in every affair and on every day of our lives, and the business of the will is to choose. But choice, the effort of decision, is a heavy labor, whether it be between two lovers or two gowns. So, many people minimize this labor by following the

---

[9]Tozer, 109.

fashion in their clothes, rooms, reading, amusements, the pictures they admire and the friends they select. We are zealous in choosing for others but shirk the responsibility of decision for ourselves.[10]

When we shirk the responsibility of decision and follow the crowd, we have made a choice. Unfortunately, when we begin reaping the consequences of those choices, the crowd runs for cover and we're left standing alone. Every moment of every day we make choices. The fact that we choose not to make thoughtful, conscious choices is still a choice.

"Choose ye this day" applies to the people we allow into our lives, into our homes, onto our TV screens, into our minds. The Bible condemns "weak-willed women" (2 Timothy 3:6) who allow people to come into their lives and lead them down the wrong path. "Choose ye this day" applies to the way we invest our time and the way we spend our money. "Choose ye this day" applies to the way we raise our children and the way we conduct our marriages. God sets the choices before us, but we must make the choice: "This day I call heaven and earth as witnesses against you that I have set before you life and death, blessings and curses. Now choose life, so that you and your children may live and that you may love the Lord your God, listen to his voice, and hold fast to him" (Deuteronomy 30:19–20).

It is precisely our will that makes us free agents. When we say God has endowed us with free will, we refer to the power of choice. However, people who are enslaved to one degree or another by "the world, the flesh and the devil" (Ephesians 2:1–3) cannot operate as free agents. We can never live in absolute freedom until "I will" becomes a more powerful force in our lives than "I want."

God gave us free wills, yet he desires us to give our will back to him. It is even as Jesus prayed in the Garden, "Yet not as I will, but as you will" (Matthew 26:39). When Jesus taught his disciples how to pray, he instructed them to first acknowledge God's holiness, and second, to declare "Thy will be done" (Matthew 6:10 KJV). It's one thing to pray that prayer and quite another to make the daily choices that will bring about God's will in and through our lives.

---

[10]Charlotte Mason, *A Philosophy of Education* (Wheaton, Ill.: Tyndale House, 1989), 131–32. (Originally published in 1925.)

Will you pray today, "Thy will be done," and then back up that prayer with right choices? Did I hear someone say, "I will"?

Reflections Along the Journey

1. Can you think of times in your life when failing to make a conscious choice led to a poor choice?

2. Which holds more sway in your life: "I want" or "I will"?

3. Write out a prayer committing to make "I will" a stronger force in your life than "I want."

4. What key lesson did you glean from today's study?

5. Write out this week's verse from memory.

Freedom Truths:

- We will live in freedom only when "I will" becomes stronger than "I want."
- God gave us a free will, yet he asks us to surrender our will to him.

Weekly Review

See if you can fill in the seven steps toward living in absolute freedom. Look in the back of the book if you need help.

F _____ your bondage

R _____ your Deliverer

E _____ your liberty

E _____ your fellow slaves

D _____ yourself in God

O _____ pockets of resistance

M _____ forward in absolute freedom

WEEK SIX:
Emancipate Your Fellow Slaves, Part One

This Week's Verse:

I, the Lord, have called you in righteousness;
I will take hold of your hand.
I will keep you and will make you
to be a covenant for the people . . .
to free captives from prison
and to release from the dungeon
those who sit in darkness.

Isaiah 42:6–7[1]

---

[1] We'll actually be working on this verse for two weeks.

Day One

Quit Messing With My Kids

Who are you to judge someone else's servant? to his own master he stands or falls. And he will stand, for the Lord is able to make him stand.

Romans 14:4

How do you feel when someone walks up to you and starts telling you how to raise your kids? Or worse, starts telling you what a lousy job you're doing? Even though, like everybody else, I *can't stand it* when someone does this to me, I occasionally succumb to the temptation to tell someone else what to do with her kids. I once *disciplined* someone else's child. Don't panic. I didn't hit the child, I just took away a toy she'd thrown across the room. Boy, was her mom mad at me! *Whew!* Another time I got into big, big, BIG trouble (you wouldn't believe how B-I-G) for *lecturing* someone else's children.

I'm learning to keep my mouth shut. Unfortunately, I'm a slow learner.

The simple fact is, people don't want you to mess with their kids.

Has it occurred to you that God feels the same way about *his* kids?

God is quite capable of lecturing his own; he doesn't need you to lecture them. God is the perfect disciplinarian; he doesn't need you to discipline his kids (except, of course, the ones he has put in *your home* for a season).

Telling everybody else what to do has been a favorite human pastime for a few millennia. It's a sport older than baseball. That doesn't mean God likes the game; he doesn't: "Who are you to judge someone else's servant? to his own master he stands or falls. And he will stand, for the Lord is able to make him stand" (Romans 14:4).

God doesn't need us to serve as his judges here on earth. He is

120

the judge, there is no other. What, then, does he want us to do in relation to others? We all know the Second Greatest Commandment: Love your neighbor as yourself. The word "love" encompasses an infinite array of attitudes and actions. But for our purposes, I'd like us to consider how we can demonstrate love by allowing others to "live in absolute freedom." Free from our evaluation. Free from our expectations. Free from our resentment. Free from our blame. Just free.

Is there a fellow believer whom you are holding in bondage? someone you've passed judgment on? someone enslaved to your high expectations? someone who dwells in the shadow of your resentment? someone held captive by the fetters of blame?

The following passage from Isaiah is Christ's job description, but in a real sense, it is our job description as well:

> This is what God the Lord says—
> he who created the heavens and
>   stretched them out,
> who spread out the earth and all that
>   comes out of it,
> who gives breath to its people,
>   and life to those who walk on it:
> "I, the Lord, have called you in righteousness;
>   I will take hold of your hand.
> I will keep you and will make you
>   to be a covenant for the people
>   and a light for the Gentiles,
> to open eyes that are blind,
>   to free captives from prison
>   and to release from the dungeon
>   those who sit in darkness" (Isaiah 42:5–7).

God is calling us to free captives from prison and release from the dungeon those who sit in darkness. I pray that God will give you the courage to unlock any prison doors to which you hold the key. You will soon discover that when you set your captives free, you'll experience a whole new level of freedom yourself.

Reflections Along the Journey

1. Can you think of a time when someone passed judgment on your

children? Describe the incident. How did it make you feel?

2. What is your reaction to the idea that when you judge a brother or a sister in Christ, you are passing judgment on God's children, and that he doesn't like it any more than you do?

3. Spend an extended time in prayer today, with a pen in hand. Ask God to show you if you are holding a fellow believer captive in any of the following areas:

You've passed judgment on someone.

You keep insisting someone has to live up to your high expectations.

You resent someone.

You blame someone.

Another form of enslavement.

4. Go back through the list. This time ask God to show you how you have enslaved yourself by enslaving others. Write any insights that come to mind.

5. Go through the list again. Ask God to show you specifically what actions you can take to "set the captives free." Note any action steps God reveals.

6. What key lesson did you glean from today's study?

Freedom Truths:

- No one wants you to "mess with her children." Neither does God want you to interfere with the discipline of his.
- We can hold others in bondage by judging, resenting, or blaming them and by setting unrealistic expectations for them to live up to.

Day Two

The Prison of Expectations

"For your Maker is your husband—
the Lord Almighty is his name—
the Holy One of Israel is your Redeemer;
he is called the God of all the earth.
The Lord will call you back
as if you were a wife deserted
and distressed in spirit—
a wife who married young,
only to be rejected," says your God.

Isaiah 54:5–6

What did you expect when you married your husband?[2]

Now *there's* a loaded question if ever I posed one!

Do you want to know what I expected when I dreamed of a husband? Why, the man on the white horse, of course! He was going to be handsome but not vain, brave but not foolish, wise but not a know-it-all, brilliant but definitely *not* smarter than me, strong but gentle, quiet but a great communicator. Get the picture?

What's that? You had a similar list?

I knew I was in trouble long before my wedding day rolled around. My husband's "charming attentiveness" had long since become "unbearable tyranny." Nevertheless, I thought we were both Christians and God could fix our marriage. After all, he had the perfect wife to work with, all he had to do was whip my husband into shape.

Our wedding night was . . . shall I say, enlightening?

Toward the end of the reception, we headed back to my house to change into our street clothes before returning for our final good-byes.

---

[2]If you are not married yet, think about what you are expecting. If you are no longer married, think about what you were expecting.

(Is it me? Or is that a really dumb tradition?) When we arrived at my house, the lights were off and the door was locked. What to do? No problem. I had been known to sneak in and out of that house many times. In fact, my bedroom window was rigged for easy escape and return. The only catch was that my bedroom was on the second floor. Again, no problem. I explained to my brand-new husband that all he had to do was get the ladder from beside the garage, lean it against my second-story window, and . . .

"I'm not going to touch that ladder!" my gallant knight replied. "I'll get grease all over my rented tuxedo." (The fact that it was a *black* tuxedo is an important footnote to this story, as you'll soon see.)

"Oh . . ." I pondered, standing there in my mother's flowing *white* wedding gown. "Ummm. Uh, well."

As I stammered and hesitated, he came up with the solution: "You're going to have to get that ladder," he declared with confidence. (You know I just love decisive men, don't you?)

Dumbfounded, I traipsed through the yard and grappled with the ladder. I managed to get it into position, then began explaining the technique for getting through the window uninjured. "It's not that hard," I assured him. "Just tuck and roll when you hit the floor."

Alas, my knight in shining armor had no intention of climbing the ladder. "I'm not climbing up there! I'm afraid of heights!" He seemed appalled that I would even suggest such a thing.

Well, you guessed it. I struggled up the ladder and crawled through the window in my mother's wedding gown, while he stood at the bottom of the ladder, unruffled, in his tuxedo. It was one of the saddest moments of my life.

Almost twenty years have passed since that night. In many ways, I've often felt like I've been climbing the ladder ever since. In the darkest moments, I've dreamed of the coveted "man on a white horse." I've dreamed of the perfect man sweeping into my life, bashing my husband upside his head and carrying me off into the sunset, never again to live in the despair of dashed expectations. I'm being brutally honest here, just as I hope you're being honest with yourself as you read along.

It was during such a time that I heard God say, "Donna, I AM the Man on the white horse. I am the lover of your soul. Let me fill those empty places in your heart. Let me be to you all the things your husband can never be; all the things *no man* could ever be."

He then laid today's passage on my heart:

> "For your Maker is your husband—
>   the Lord Almighty is his name—
> the Holy One of Israel is your Redeemer;
>   he is called the God of all the earth.
> The Lord will call you back
>   as if you were a wife deserted and
>   distressed in spirit—
> a wife who married young,
>   only to be rejected," says your God.

My friend Teresa Taylor has written a marvelous song that sums up the message of that passage. It's called "Perfect Man":[3]

> Looking every day for Mr. Right,
> crying all alone late in the night,
> till one day I finally realized
> that I found the perfect man
> right before my eyes,
> and there'll never be another perfect man,
> no, there'll never be another perfect man.
> Oh, you gotta fill that hunger in your soul,
> searching for someone to make you whole,
> but only Jesus' love will make you complete,
> and you can find yourself down at his feet.
> When you're looking for love and true affection—
> well, don't be looking for perfection.
> A perfect man you will never find
> 'cause there's only been One since the dawn of time,
> and there will never be another Perfect Man.
> © 1999 Teresa Wright Taylor & Jeff McCullough.
> Teresa Taylor Tunes. ASCAP.

When God, the Perfect Man, becomes your husband, you can set your husband free to be imperfect. When you turn your heart completely to the One who will never disappoint you, you can set your

---

[3]Used by permission. This song is recorded on Teresa's debut album, *Purple Heart*. It also features my all-time favorite Christian song, "Cha-Cha-Cha." To order a copy, contact Teresa Taylor, P.O. Box 423, Temecula, CA 92593, (909) 678–5060.

husband free to disappoint you. When you cling to the One who said, "I will never leave you nor forsake you," you can set free the one who has left you, whether he has left you physically—or emotionally. Let God be your husband.

Reflections Along the Journey

1. What were your expectations when you entered marriage?

2. How has your spouse failed to meet those expectations? (Don't write a twenty-page essay!)

3. How would your marriage be different if you set your husband free to disappoint you?

4. How would your marriage be different if you allowed God to become to you all those things that your husband can't be?

5. What are some practical ways that you can enter into the truth that "Your Maker is your husband"?

6. Write a prayer expressing your love for the Perfect Man.

7. What key lesson did you glean from today's study?

Freedom Truths:

- There will never be another Perfect Man.
- Set your husband free to disappoint you—and let God become to you all that your husband cannot be.

Day Three

Stop the Blame Game

Some of you may not have been able to relate to yesterday's message. Maybe your husband surpasses your expectations. Or maybe you're single. Maybe you're divorced or widowed. Not to fear. Today we have something for everyone, because although we don't all have husbands, we all have someone to *blame*.

Do you know what's wrong with me? (Did I hear someone say, "Lots of things"?) Seriously, do you know what's wrong with me? My parents messed me up. I mean that literally. My mom let me keep my room a mess, and that's why my house is a wreck. My dad never wanted me to work (he grew up during the Depression and never did anything *but* work), and that's why I'm so lazy.

Do you know why I'm so obnoxiously insecure? It's those rotten kids I went to school with. You may even be wondering why I'm a junk-food junkie. Easy, that's my brothers' and sisters' fault. They always gobbled down all the junk food before I could get any, and that made me paranoid about getting my share.

I could go on. . . .

It's called the Blame Game. Ever play it?

The first professional players were Adam and Eve:

> When the woman saw that the fruit of the tree was good for food and pleasing to the eye, and also desirable for gaining wisdom, she took some and ate it. She also gave some to her husband, who was with her, and he ate it. Then the eyes of both of them were opened, and they realized they were naked; so they sewed fig leaves together and made coverings for themselves.
>
> Then the man and his wife heard the sound of the Lord God as he was walking in the garden in the cool of the day, and they hid from the Lord God among the trees of the garden. But the Lord God called to the man, "Where are you?"

He answered, "I heard you in the garden, and I was afraid because I was naked; so I hid."

And he said, "Who told you that you were naked? Have you eaten from the tree that I commanded you not to eat from?"

The man said, "The woman you put here with me—she gave me some fruit from the tree, and I ate it."

Then the Lord God said to the woman, "What is this you have done?"

The woman said, "The serpent deceived me, and I ate" (Genesis 3:6–13).

Let's see here. It was Eve's fault. No, it was the serpent's fault. Actually, it was God's fault. What happened to that stuff about "no temptation has seized you except what is common to man"? I mean, this fruit test was more than anyone could bear.

I've played the Blame Game my whole life. At times I've let it consume me. Since my greatest failures are on the home front, that's where most of the action takes place. I know for a fact that if my mom had been the perfect mom, I'd be a better mom. It's all her fault that I'll never be Martha Stewart. Even so, if I had different kids, I could still be a great mom. It's their fault that I'm a raging lunatic. Besides, I'm a homeschooling mom. It's because of homeschooling. As I'm fond of saying: "If it weren't for my kids, I would love home-schooling. And if it weren't for homeschooling, I would love my kids."

So, anybody else want to play? Anyone who *doesn't* want to play—but finds herself playing anyway?

To tell you the truth, after almost forty years of playing, I have to admit, the game is getting a little old. I've been seriously thinking about taking responsibility for my own life. And if I had better parents, I would have taken responsibility long ago. Oops! Seriously, it's time to set the captives free. It's time to stop blaming other people for being human and start facing our own humanity in the process.

This may sound weird coming from a Christian author, but I'm continually disappointed by my *own* Christian walk. I wish I were much stronger than I am, much further along the path of righteousness. All blaming aside, I *do* believe that those who have been blessed with a Christian heritage have a tremendous advantage in life. If you were given such a gift, don't apologize for it. Someone, somewhere paid the price that you might inherit a blessing. Maybe it was your mother, your grandmother, your great-grandmother. But the fact is, Satan doesn't give up his territory without a fight. Sometimes people raised in wonderful Christian homes will come up to me and say apologetically, "Gee, I don't have an amazing testimony like you." To which I respond, "Having a testimony is just a polite way of saying I've made a mess of my life. Believe me, you wouldn't want to trade places with me."

I can't change the past.

But praise God, I can change the future. I can give to my children the greatest gift any parent can bestow: a godly heritage. Following is the verse God laid on my heart for my daughter Taraneh:

> They will be called oaks of
> righteousness,
> a planting of the Lord
> for the display of his splendor.
> They will rebuild the ancient ruins
> and restore the places long
> devastated;
> they will renew the ruined cities
> that have been devastated for
> generations.
> Their descendants will be known
> among the nations
> and their offspring among the
> peoples.
> All who see them will acknowledge
> that they are a people the Lord has
> blessed.
> (Isaiah 61:3b–4, 9)

OK, now read it again.

I said, read it again! (I can't remember whose fault it is that I'm so bossy!)

Here's where I'm at: I'm done digging up the past. I'm done searching for skeletons in the closet. I've decided to set my "family of origin" free. I'm not going to blame them for my shortcomings anymore. And I'm certainly not going to blame them for how my children turn out. Starting today, I am taking absolute responsibility before

God to do all I can to see these promises come to fruition in the next generation.

If you are ready to join me in that commitment, then pray along:

Lord, I believe that my children will be called oaks of righteousness, that they will be strong in their walk. I believe that my children are a planting of the Lord for the display of your splendor. I believe that you will be glorified in their lives. Lord, I ask that you will enable them to rebuild the ancient ruins and restore the places long devastated. I pray that you will empower them to overcome generational curses—patterns of sin that have haunted my family. I pray that I will live to see the day when they renew those places of heart, mind, and soul that have been devastated for generations.

And Father, I dare to ask for even more. I ask that their descendants will be known among the nations and their offspring among the peoples. More than anything else, I pray that all who see them will acknowledge that they are a people the Lord has blessed. May it be so. Amen and Amen.

Reflections Along the Journey

1. Make a list of all the problems in your life for which you blame other people:

Problem   **Person You Blame**

Some of you may need to continue on a separate page. That's OK. Let God direct this exercise.[4]

2. Now bring your list before the Lord and begin to pray. Ask God to enable you to "release your captives," to set them free from all blame.

3. How has releasing others from blame set *you* free to move on with your life?

4. What key lesson did you glean from today's study?

Freedom Truths:

- No one has ever won the Blame Game.
- You can't change the past, but you can change the future.

---

[4]If you struggle in this area, I would strongly encourage you to read my book *Walking in Total God-Confidence*. I believe it will help you work through many of the issues that underlie the Blame Game.

Day Four

Setting the Captives Free Through Forgiveness

Forgiveness is setting the prisoner free. Then realizing that the prisoner was me.

Today I want to share with you a spiritual insight that you will not find revealed elsewhere in the annals of Christendom. It took me seventeen years to figure out this insight, which is so profound I'm thinking about printing T-shirts with this slogan emblazoned on them:

God Is Bigger Than the Jerks

Well, what do you think?

What's that? You want to place an order?

Perhaps you object to my use of the word "jerk" in a Christian book. Don't worry. It is a biblical term. It's from the Greek *Jerkolopolis*.

God is bigger than the jerks! He's bigger than all the jerks in the world combined. In fact, a whole planet full of jerks cannot thwart God's plan for our lives. Do you know that? God is in control. See, I always thought that God had a plan, but the jerks came along and blew the whole thing to pieces. Now, don't get me wrong. I'm not saying God deliberately sends the jerks. No, not at all. God does not send the jerks, but he sure puts them to good use molding our character.

Maybe your husband, or your kids, or your parents, or your boss, or people in your church are acting like real jerks. And you think: *How can I be what God wants me to be when they're standing in the way?*

Philippians 1:6 says we can be confident of this: "that he who began a good work in you will carry it on to completion." There's not a jerk in the world who can prevent God from carrying that good work to completion. And what exactly *is* that good work?

134

It's the work of transforming our character. God's purpose for our lives is that we would truly become women of virtue. His ultimate plan for our lives has very little to do with our circumstances. Those are just the tools he uses to transform us into a vessel he can use. Whether it's physical illness or financial difficulties. Whether you're single and you wish you were married. Or married and you wish you were single. The circumstances aren't the point.

And by the way, God's ultimate plan has nothing to do with our convenience, although you wouldn't think so by looking at most of our prayer lists. It has to do with our character. And there's nothing quite like a jerk to drive us to our knees as we allow God to transform us from the inside out. As you can see, jerks actually play a vital role in our spiritual growth.

Let's hear it for the jerks!

All kidding aside. I want to talk with you very personally for a moment. Chances are if you've been on the planet for more than a week you've encountered a jerk. Someone who has hurt you very deeply. And you're harboring that right to be hurt like a prized possession.

It's time to let it go.

It's time to forgive.

Now you're objecting, *If you knew what a jerk he was, you wouldn't ask me to forgive him.* You're absolutely right. I don't know. But God does, and he is the one asking you to forgive. Forgive because God first forgave you. Forgive because forgiving doesn't make them right, forgiving sets you free. Forgive because it cleanses the bitterness, and God cannot use a vessel filled with bitterness.

I've also observed that the motivating force behind most jerks is their desire to control. They want power over you. Now think about this for a moment: As long as you don't forgive, they are in control. As long as you don't forgive, you're giving them exactly what they wanted in the first place.

Forgive, and give God control of your life again.

Reflections Along the Journey

1. Is there a jerk in your life? Describe what effect you've allowed him or her to have upon your life.

2. What are the implications in your life of the "profound spiritual insight" that God is bigger than the jerks?

3. Who do you need to forgive?

4. Write out your prayer of forgiveness.

5. What key lesson did you glean from today's study?

Freedom Truths:

- God is bigger than the jerks.
- Forgiving doesn't make the jerk right; forgiving sets you free.
- Forgive, and give God control of your life.

Day Five

They're Making Me Sin

Do you have people in your life who *make you sin?*
I know I do!

Do you want to know who they are? My KIDS!!!

I suppose the mere fact that we're together twenty-four hours a day causes me to find them . . . dare I say it? Annoying. It's tempting to think, *If I could just ship these kids off to boarding school, I would be a saint.* (Wait a minute. Boarding school?! Not a bad idea.) It's tempting to point the finger at the little urchins and yell, "You kids are making me sin!" When I feel that way, I'm not only angry with them for what they *did or did not do,* I'm angry with them for how they are *making me* feel and act.

See, they are *making me* feel like a nut. They are *making me* act like a lunatic. I'm enslaved to their actions. Or am I?

One day it occurred to me that I don't have to be enslaved to their actions. I don't have to let what they do determine how I feel and what I do. What a liberating moment! I realized, they're not making me sin. They're just revealing the sin that's already there.

Think about that for a minute.

Maybe you've been telling yourself, *If I had a different husband, I would be the perfect wife. If I had different kids, I'd be the mother of the year. If I had a different boss, I'd be a great employee.* However, we're just deceiving ourselves. The truth is, we're sinners in need of repentance. A different husband might make our lives less tumultuous, but it wouldn't do a thing to change the condition of our heart.

Rather than living in bondage to other people's actions and attitudes, allow God to use those very same actions and attitudes to set you free—free from the power of sin in your life. Difficult people can actually play a tremendous role in our spiritual growth if we respond properly. Here's how the process works:

1. *REVEAL*—the first step to cleansing is revelation. You can't be cleansed of a sin if you don't know it exists. So people who anger or hurt you actually provide a great service when they reveal the sin within.

2. *CONFESS*—the next step is the key: Once the sin is revealed, we must confess it. As far as I have been able to determine, nowhere in the Bible does God promise to forgive unconfessed sin. Remember 1 John 1:9: "If we confess our sins, he is faithful and just to forgive us our sins and purify us from all unrighteousness." Which do you think is the most important word in that verse? In my opinion, it's that tiny two-letter word "if."

3. *CLEANSE*—once *other people* have done their part in revealing our sin, and once we've done our part in confessing our sin, then and only then can God do his part of cleansing the sin.

Now I want you to sit down and write a thank-you note to the most difficult person you know. You don't have to lie. Just write, "I want to thank you for the vital role you're playing in my spiritual growth."

Reflections Along the Journey

1. How can the realization that difficult people actually play an important role in your spiritual growth change your attitude toward them?

2. What are some sins that difficult people have revealed in your life?

3. Write out a prayer confessing those sins to God and asking him to cleanse you.

4. What key lesson did you glean from today's study?

Freedom Truths:

- Difficult people play an important part in our spiritual growth—they reveal the sin in our hearts.
- Once the sin is revealed, we can then confess it and be cleansed of it.

Weekly Review

See if you can fill in the seven steps toward living in absolute freedom. Look in the back of the book if you need help.

F_____ your bondage

R_____ your Deliverer

E_____ your liberty

E_____ your fellow slaves

D_____ yourself in God

O_____ pockets of resistance

M_____ forward in absolute freedom

WEEK SEVEN:
Emancipate Your Fellow Slaves, Part Two

This Week's Verse:

I, the Lord, have called you in righteousness;
I will take hold of your hand.
I will keep you and will make you
to be a covenant for the people . . .
to free captives from prison
and to release from the dungeon
those who sit in darkness.

Isaiah 42:6–7

Day One

The Broken Places, Part One

This is the most important week of our journey. This isn't one you can skim through and "get the gist" of things. It's been my observation from the study of Scripture and church history that whenever God wants to intervene in human history, he does two very simple things. First, he chooses the *wrong person*, then he follows that up with a really *dumb idea*. Today we'll see this evidenced in the life of Gideon. Please carefully read the following passages from Judges 6 and 7:

> The angel of the Lord came and sat down under the oak in Ophrah that belonged to Joash the Abiezrite, where his son Gideon was threshing wheat in a winepress to keep it from the Midianites. When the angel of the Lord appeared to Gideon, he said, "The Lord is with you, mighty warrior."
>
> "But sir," Gideon replied, "if the Lord is with us, why has all this happened to us? Where are all his wonders that our fathers told us about when they said, 'Did not the Lord bring us up out of Egypt?' But now the Lord has abandoned us and put us into the hand of Midian."
>
> The Lord turned to him and said, "Go in the strength you have and save Israel out of Midian's hand. Am I not sending you?"
>
> "But LORD," Gideon asked, "how can I save Israel? My clan is the weakest in Manasseh, and I am the least in my family."
>
> The Lord answered, "I will be with you, and you will strike down all the Midianites together" (Judges 6:11–16).
>
> Early in the morning, Jerub-Baal (that is, Gideon) and all his men camped at the spring of Harod. The camp of Midian was north of them in the valley near the hill of Moreh. The Lord said to Gideon, "You have too many men for me to deliver Midian into their hands. In order that Israel may not boast against me that

her own strength has saved her, announce now to the people, 'Anyone who trembles with fear may turn back and leave Mount Gilead.'" So twenty-two thousand men left, while ten thousand remained.

But the Lord said to Gideon, "There are still too many men. Take them down to the water, and I will sift them for you there. If I say, 'This one shall go with you,' he shall go; but if I say, 'This one shall not go with you,' he shall not go."

So Gideon took the men down to the water. There the Lord told him, "Separate those who lap the water with their tongues like a dog from those who kneel down to drink." Three hundred men lapped with their hands to their mouths. All the rest got down on their knees to drink.

The Lord said to Gideon, "With the three hundred men that lapped I will save you and give the Midianites into your hands. Let all the other men go, each to his own place." So Gideon sent the rest of the Israelites to their tents but kept the three hundred, who took over the provisions and trumpets of the others.

Now the camp of Midian lay below him in the valley. During that night the Lord said to Gideon, "Get up, go down against the camp, because I am going to give it into your hands. If you are afraid to attack, go down to the camp with your servant Purah and listen to what they are saying. Afterward, you will be encouraged to attack the camp." So he and Purah his servant went down to the outposts of the camp. The Midianites, the Amalekites and all the other eastern peoples had settled in the valley, thick as locusts. Their camels could no more be counted than the sand on the seashore.

Gideon arrived just as a man was telling a friend his dream. "I had a dream," he was saying. "A round loaf of barley bread came tumbling into the Midianite camp. It struck the tent with such force that the tent overturned and collapsed."

His friend responded, "This can be nothing other than the sword of Gideon son of Joash, the Israelite. God has given the Midianites and the whole camp into his hands."

When Gideon heard the dream and its interpretation, he worshiped God. He returned to the camp of Israel and called out, "Get up! The Lord has given the Midianite camp into your hands." Dividing the three hundred men into three companies, he placed trumpets and empty jars in the hands of all of them, with torches inside.

"Watch me," he told them. "Follow my lead. When I get to the edge of the camp, do exactly as I do. When I and all who are with me blow our trumpets, then from all around the camp blow yours and shout, 'For the Lord and for Gideon.' "

Gideon and the hundred men with him reached the edge of the camp at the beginning of the middle watch, just after they had changed the guard. They blew their trumpets and broke the jars that were in their hands. The three companies blew the trumpets and smashed the jars. Grasping the torches in their left hands and holding in their right hands the trumpets they were to blow, they shouted, "A sword for the Lord and for Gideon!" While each man held his position around the camp, all the Midianites ran, crying out as they fled. When the three hundred trumpets sounded, the Lord caused the men throughout the camp to turn on each other with their swords" (Judges 7:1–22).

Tomorrow I'm going to make some observations about this passage. For today, I want you to make your *own* observations:

1. How valid do you consider Gideon's objections to God's selection of him?
2. What do you think was going through Gideon's mind when God told him he had too many men?
3. Is there such a thing as *too many on your side* when you go into battle? How can that be so?
4. Why do you think God wanted to "winnow down" the number of soldiers?
5. What do you make of the weapons God provided?
6. What do you think is the significance of the way the battle was waged?
7. Who received the credit for the victory?
8. Why should it matter who gets the credit?
9. Can you think of any applications of these passages to your own life? Are there any battles you are facing in which these principles of warfare might apply?

Reflections Along the Journey

1. You already did your reflecting for today, but feel free to jot down any wrap-up thoughts that spring to mind.

2. What key lesson did you glean from today's study?

Freedom Truths:

- It's possible for us to set up our lives in such a way that God cannot work effectively.
- God goes to great lengths to ensure that he gets the credit for the battles he wins.

Day Two

The Broken Places, Part Two

Yesterday you spent time making your own observations on the passages from Judges 6 and 7. Today it's my turn. First, I notice that God has successfully managed to choose the wrong person. This is a sure sign that we're on the verge of witnessing a God thing. (A God thing is something only God can do!) Gideon is obviously a bit of a wimp. He is attempting to thresh wheat—something that needs to be done out in an open field—down in a winepress. Why? Because he is hiding from his enemies. That's why there's more than a bit of irony in the angel's greeting: "mighty warrior." But I think the greeting also demonstrates that God sees Gideon not only for who he is at the moment but also as the person he can become.

This man of faith is obviously lacking faith in the midst of his current circumstances as he questions God's goodness and point-blank accuses him of abandoning his people. Gideon also tells us that he is unqualified for leadership: he's the youngest in his family, and his family is from the weakest tribe.

OK, great. We've got the wrong person. All that's lacking is the really dumb idea. Here it comes: God deliberately "winnows" an army of 32,000 men down to 300. God does this because he is very concerned about his glory. He is concerned that Gideon and his men will claim the victory for themselves, that they will steal his glory if they possibly can. That's why God is determined to winnow the army down to a miniscule number so that there is absolutely no way any human being can take the credit for something God has done.

For too long the church has been stealing God's glory. We've become so confident about our church-growth methods, so proud of our size and success, God doesn't even need to show up for the service. In our private lives, the message of the church has been: Get your life together so you can impress your neighbors and co-workers into the kingdom. When they see how wonderful you are they'll want to "have what you have."

The church worships sports heroes and beauty queens, holding them up as examples of successful Christian lives. Of course, the rationalization is that these superstars can then *share their glory* with God. Gee, how lucky can God get?! God isn't in the business of sharing his glory. In fact, he will not share his glory with another.

Well, we've got the dumb idea going now and we understand why. But apparently God doesn't think it's dumb enough. After all, 300 men can still do a lot of bragging. I mean, if you've got a husband, you know how much bragging ONE man can do. Now multiply that by 300 and you can see why God is concerned. So God runs with an idea that is truly ludicrous. He sends 300 men into battle equipped with a trumpet, a torch, and a jar of clay. This is not smart warfare. The torch and the jar of clay don't make any sense at all. The trumpet, of course, is for any surviving soldiers to play "Taps" in honor of everyone else who is sure to be slaughtered.

Often God sends us into situations that we feel ill-equipped to confront. Good! That way we'll rely on God rather than on our equipment.

However, I think the most remarkable aspect of this story is how God secures the victory: He commands the soldiers to smash their jars of clay and allow the radiance from their torches to shine forth. And when they do, the enemies of God are scattered without a shot being fired.

Second Corinthians 4:7 says, "We have this treasure in jars of clay to show that the all-surpassing power is from God and not from us." Like Gideon's soldiers, God has sent us onto the battlefield of life equipped with only three things: a trumpet—our voice to proclaim the truth; a jar of clay—our physical bodies, in which God dwells; and a torch—the radiance of God igniting our hearts.

When God allows us, as jars of clay, to be *smashed* by the blows of life, it is then that *his* glory shines forth into a darkened world.

Tomorrow I'll explain exactly how that process takes place.

Reflections Along the Journey

1. Can you see the advantage to the kingdom of God when God deliberately chooses the "wrong person" to work through?

2. Do you feel like you are the "wrong person" for God to work through?

3. Why did God winnow down Gideon's army?

4. Has God done any "winnowing down" in your life? in the life of your church?

5. What do you think "God will not share his glory with another" means?

6. In what ways have you stolen God's glory in your life?

7. What key lesson did you glean from today's study?

Freedom Truths:

- Sometimes God deliberately "winnows us down" to ensure that we do not steal his glory.
- God sends us forth onto the battlefield of life equipped only with our voice and the radiance of his glory.

Day Three

Redeeming the Broken Places

There's a lot we can do with the broken places in our lives: we can glue them back together; we can try to cover them up; we can decorate them: maybe slap on some paint or fabric or wallpaper; we can turn the broken places back toward the wall so no one will notice them.

I could have done that on the pages of this book: covered up, hidden the truth. And you would have been none the wiser! I mean, I could have fooled y'all quite easily. You would have finished this book thinking, *Wow, that Donna is amazing! What a spiritual giant! I could never be like her.* Who would have gotten the glory? Me.

When God called me into public ministry, I thought, *Okay, all I have to do is cover up the cracks. I'll keep the broken places in my life a secret, then God will be able to use me* in spite of *the stupid choices I've made*, in spite of *the problems I grapple with.* So I pretended that everything was just fine in my life—and my ministry was mediocre. Oh sure, I got up with a microphone and talked. People applauded politely. But very few lives were changed.

Not surprisingly God refused to bless my little game show. For nearly two solid years the only message God would speak to my heart was "I will not share my glory with another. I will not share my glory with *you*."

And so on the pages of this book I have revealed to you the broken places in my life. I've told you that I routinely blow it as a wife, as a mom, and as a follower of Christ. NEVERTHELESS, God is able to work through my life to bring glory to himself.

You see, having read this book thus far, you can only reach one conclusion: *If God can set* that woman *free, surely he can set me free too. If God can minister through* her life, *surely he can minister through mine.*

It took me a long time, but I finally realized: God does not want to be glorified in my life *in spite of my weaknesses*. He wants to be glorified in my life *because of my weaknesses*. That's what the Bible means when it says, " 'My grace is sufficient for you, *for my power is made perfect in weakness.*' Therefore I [Paul] will boast all the more gladly about my weaknesses, so that Christ's power may rest on me. That is why, for Christ's sake, I delight in weaknesses, in insults, in hardships, in persecutions, in difficulties. For when I am weak, then I am strong" (2 Corinthians 12:9–10).

What are the broken places in your life? Something you wish were different, something you wish had never happened. You have a choice, right at this moment. You can cover the broken place, or you can allow God to be glorified through it. Here's the way I think of it: Imagine that your broken place is a coupon—like the one you cut out of the newspaper. But if it lays around, hidden away in the kitchen drawer, it is absolutely useless. Then one day you make a decision: you take out that coupon, march down to the grocery store, and hand it over with your purchase to the cashier. You give it to someone who has the power and authority to redeem it—the power and authority to take something that is absolutely worthless by itself and transform it into something valuable. We're talking triple-bonus coupon here.

That's what God is calling you to do with that broken place in your life. It's useless hidden away in some junk drawer in your heart. Take it out. Hand that worthless piece of brokenness over to God. Hand it over to the One who has the power and authority to take something that is absolutely worthless and transform it into something valuable.

If I had not let God redeem my broken places—my mistakes, my heartaches—I don't think I could go on living. When I think about my past, all the pain I've lived through, the only thing that enables me to press on is the realization that God is daily redeeming all that broken stuff. Even as you read these words today, God is redeeming a broken place in my heart. I figure if what I've lived through can make a difference in one person's life, then it wasn't in vain.

Although I wouldn't wish my choices on my worst enemy, I refuse to live consumed by regret. When a woman comes to me grappling with depression, I can pray with her and she *knows* that I know. And she sees that I'm still standing, that life can go on. . . . Wow! I can't even tell you what joy floods my heart. When I talk on the phone with a woman who is struggling in her marriage, a woman whose husband is acting like a real jerk, and I can point her to the truth of God's Word—the truth that God himself is her husband—and I hear her, long distance, grabbing hold of that truth. . . . Wow! I see the glory! I see the glory!

People will sometimes ask me, "How can I know what ministry God is calling me to? I want to serve him, but I'm not sure how or where." I always tell them: Look to your broken places.

What are the broken places in your life? Those are your opportunities for ministry. It is through them that God wants to shine forth his glory to a darkened world.

Reflections Along the Journey

1. What are some of the broken places in your life?

2. How have you tried to handle them: by hiding them? decorating them? ignoring them?

3. As you consider possible opportunities for ministry, what clues do you discover by looking to your broken places?

4. What key lesson did you glean from today's study?

Freedom Truths:

- If you're trying to discover your place of ministry, look to your broken places.
- God wants to shine forth his glory through you to a darkened world.

Day Four

Her Broken Place

As I was writing this week's lessons, I knew I was going to share a song by Teresa Taylor. So, for fun, I called her and asked if she had a copy of her testimony I could share with you. Realize she did not write it *for this book*; it's just a reflection of the work God has been doing in her life. When I read it, it boggled my mind how God has been teaching her *the very same truths* he's been teaching me and that I, in turn, have been teaching you. No wonder her music has ministered to me so powerfully. Watch this:

> I asked Jesus to come into my heart when I was five years old. But unfortunately, He never got the chance to really move in and settle down, because at age seven I hung this "Closed" sign on the door of my heart the day my grandfather molested me. That was the day I came to believe I couldn't trust anyone. I thought I was on my own from there on out, and I learned to survive by my wits alone. I locked the door on the emotions of that little girl and left her there in the dark for years.
>
> Last September the healing process took a giant leap when I felt that God wanted me to really open up and start sharing my story. You know that you really have true healing when you can freely talk about a painful place in your life and it doesn't hurt anymore. This has been the most liberating experience of my life. He is setting me free from the fear of rejection, not only from others, but of rejecting myself. He's showing me how to accept myself and to see myself as He sees me. He is showing me how opening up my heart and hanging this "Open" sign on the door can be the most incredible thing. *And through His love, I can take my pain and make it gain for myself and for you. And that's why I'm sharing a part of my life with you today* [emphasis added].
>
> Because I believed I couldn't trust anyone, I spent a lot of time alone. I began taking piano lessons in second grade, and that

was my perfect excuse for solitude. I could spend all that time practicing and becoming good at something, and no one would be the wiser. No one would know there was anything wrong with me. Music became my only emotional release. The piano was my best friend. I could hide behind my musical talent, and I did hide there for many years.

I spent my teenage years looking for love in all the wrong places. I was looking for someone to help me feel better about myself, someone to say, "There's nothing wrong with you. You're perfect. You're the girl of my dreams. I love you." The innocent little girl was looking for someone she could trust.

That little girl was still alone when, in college, I found the perfect guy: a big, strong idealist who stood up for what he believed. I knew he was the one to save me from myself. He was studying to be a minister. I was studying music. I would make the perfect preacher's wife. We were a perfect match.

During the early years of our marriage, we had two children. And because of my pregnancy weight gain, I became buried more and more under a mountain of depression. I ate my way to well over two hundred pounds. The more I ate, the worse I felt about myself. I felt isolated and alone.

We were starting a church at that time in Temecula [California], and this seemed like the worst time in my life. How could I be a pastor's wife and help other people, and love other people, when I hated myself? I was at the bottom. I had sunk so low I wouldn't leave the house for days at a time. I could barely drag myself to church on Sunday. I functioned in daily life purely on a mental level, not wanting to deal with the emotional pit deep inside me.

I had been raised to believe that as long as everything was okay on the outside, then I would be fine. So, finally, after a couple years of this depression, I knew that if I didn't change, I wouldn't survive. I decided to lose weight and I did. I lost ninety pounds over a three-year period by sheer willpower and discipline. I thought that surely this would solve all my problems. But soon after that, I learned differently.

I still hadn't learned to open up and trust anyone, even my husband. And my world was shaken when he became unsure of his beliefs and began to wrestle with his own insecurities and inner turmoil. How could he save me from myself when he was not so "perfect" anymore? The little girl was still hiding there the day he said, "I can't say that I love you anymore," and he moved out.

At first, I denied that any of this was my fault. He was the one with all the problems. I was getting my life on the right track. I was looking good and I was feeling good. He needed to just get his act together. But really I was too afraid to look in my heart. I knew it would be like opening Pandora's box. There were too many skeletons lurking in that closet. I didn't want to accept the fact that what had happened to me twenty years before had caused me to ruin so many relationships in my life, including the most important relationship I could have with someone.

During this time I was beginning to lead praise and worship at my church more, and was asked to lead other places. It was through this time of turmoil that God found the chink in my armor. I would open the door to Him when I would sing and worship, but I would only let Him in so far. It was the same love for music that I used to shut out the world that He used to get in my heart.

So month after month He gently worked His way through all my mess and all the darkness in my heart. Slowly I began to let Him shine His light in every little corner, exposing all my big fears for the little things that they really were. They were just casting big shadows in the darkness. But when He turned the light on, they were so small and insignificant. It was like being afraid of a Pit Bull next door all your life only to find out it was a Poodle.

He is now teaching me to be intimate with Him and with others. Intimacy—"into me see." He's teaching me how to be vulnerable and how much strength there is in vulnerability. He's promised to restore my innocence by healing that little girl inside me and bringing joy where there was pain, and bringing a sense of wonder where there was hopelessness. He's restoring my relationship with my husband and allowing us to have a new beginning. He's giving me a chance to direct the anger that I felt at myself and those who have hurt me and to put it in the right place, which is to take what Satan meant for evil and bring good out of it. And He's showing me how that by helping you who have been through similar hurts and pains, and by just saying, "Hey, God was there for me and He'll be there for you, too," the simplicity of that not only brings encouragement to you but also encourages me and brings me the "peace that passes all understanding."

Reflections Along the Journey

1. What "broken place" principles did you notice in Teresa's story?

2. Was God able to glorify himself through those broken places? How so?

3. Was God able to minister to your heart through Teresa's broken places? Describe.

4. Write out a prayer asking God to reveal your broken places.

5. What key lesson did you glean from today's study?

Freedom Truths:

- We can spend our entire lives living in fear of the Pit Bull next door when it's actually a Poodle.
- God is calling us to intimacy: "into me see."

Day Five

The Ceremony

Yesterday we saw how Teresa has given the broken pieces in her life to the One who can redeem them. Today it's your turn. If you are doing this study as part of a group, I would encourage you to do the following ceremony together. Otherwise, you can do it alone before the Lord.

1. Gather together two lightweight terra-cotta pots, a pen or felt-tip marker, a hammer, a freestanding candle, and a match. Place the lighted candle under the terra-cotta pot. If you can darken the room, so much the better. (Have a flashlight for the person who will read the Scripture passage.)

2. Read the passage from Judges 7. When Gideon's army smash their jars of clay, crack the terra-cotta pot just enough for the light to shine through.

3. Next, smash the second terra-cotta pot into small pieces.

4. Now begin to pray, asking God to show you the broken places in your life. As God brings places to mind, write them down on one of the small pieces of clay. You may use a separate piece of clay for each broken place. (Note: If you are doing this in a group, make sure there are enough broken pieces for each person to receive at least one. You might want to smash the pieces in advance or have more than two pots to ensure you have enough.)

5. Now place the broken pieces alongside the cracked pot, as you ask God to redeem them and use them to minister to others.

6. Finally, overturn the cracked pot and place your broken places inside of it. If you are doing this alone, you can keep this as a permanent remembrance of your commitment to God.

7. Extinguish the flame.

8. From time to time, review your broken places in a time of prayer and recommitment. You may want to light your candle during

these times as a reminder that the purpose is that God's glory might shine forth through your life to a darkened world.

Often after doing this ceremony at a retreat, I will spend time on my knees, praying over the broken places. As I have looked upon the words scribbled on these pieces of clay, it almost invariably boils down to the issue of forgiveness. People need to forgive others—and they need to forgive themselves.

Usually when we're through with the ceremony at women's retreats, everyone's a-cryin'. So sometimes I like to spring something fun on them, and the next thing you know, everyone's a-flyin'. This might sound crazy, and maybe it is, but I like to share a favorite song. It's by Teresa Taylor, and it's called "Cha-Cha-Cha." And now that we've all been set free from legalism, I'll let you in on a little secret: I've been known to lead a conga line[1] of set-free ladies at the end of the retreat. Try it at your Bible study this week. It's a hoot.

OK, get ready for my theme song:

CHA-CHA-CHA[2]

Jesus took my sadness
and he turned it into gladness.
He gave me a new life
and a new chance,
and it makes me wanna dance.
Cha-Cha-Cha!
'Cause I'm so happy!
He gave me health;
He gave me strength;
He gave me breath;
I gotta sing.
He gave me feet,
He gave me hands.
I gotta clap;
I gotta dance.
Whoa, yeah!

---

[1] Conga is a Cuban dance of African origin involving three steps followed by a kick and performed by a group usually in single file following a leader.

[2] If you are ready for some serious freedom in your group, call Teresa Taylor and get a copy of her CD featuring the "Cha-Cha-Cha" song. I warn you, though, it is WILD. (909) 678–5060.

He gave me faith;
He gave me hope;
He gave me love;
I gotta show.
He gave me joy;
He gave me peace;
I gotta shout:
He set me free!
© 1999 Teresa Wright Taylor & Jeff McCullough.
Teresa Taylor Tunes. ASCAP.

Reflections Along the Journey

1. Write out a prayer, turning that broken place in your life over to
   God and expressing your willingness to allow him to redeem it and
   use it to bring glory to himself.

2. Walk through the steps of the "Broken Places Ceremony" (either
   privately or with your small group) and note your reaction to the
   experience.

3. What key lesson did you glean from today's study?

4. Write out this week's verse from memory.

Freedom Truths:

- It's through the broken places in our lives that God wants to show forth his glory.
- God wants to redeem the broken places in your life.

Weekly Review

See if you can fill in the seven steps toward living in absolute freedom. Look in the back of the book if you need help,

F _____ your bondage

R _____ your Deliverer

E _____ your liberty

E _____ your fellow slaves

D _____ yourself in God

O _____ pockets of resistance

M_____ forward in absolute freedom

WEEK EIGHT:
Delight Yourself in God

This Week's Verse:

Delight yourself in the Lord
and he will give you the desires of your heart.
Commit your way to the Lord;
trust in him and he will do this:
He will make your righteousness shine like the dawn,
the justice of your cause like the noonday sun.

Psalm 37:4–6

Day One

Delight Yourself in God

Delight yourself in the Lord
  and he will give you the desires of your heart.
Commit your way to the Lord;
  trust in him and he will do this:
He will make your righteousness shine like the dawn,
  the justice of your cause like the noonday sun.

Psalm 37:4–6

My husband performs a little ritual each night before our three-year-old daughter, Taraneh, goes to bed. Throughout the household, everyone knows when the ritual is underway, because we can hear Tara's squeals of delight. Sometimes we all pile into bed with her to watch the show. Last night was such a night. I was cuddling up behind Tara, delighting in her delight, when she suddenly nudged me and said indignantly: "Mommy, you HAVE to go _____." (Fill in a squealing sound. I can't figure out how to translate it!) It wasn't enough for me to be a bystander, an uninvolved witness; she wanted me to enter into her delight.

By now you're probably wondering, *What exactly is this delightful ritual all about?* Well, how can I put this? My husband stands outside Tara's doorway, puts a towel on his head, then leans into the room, makes a silly face, and quickly pulls his head back out of the room. He does this over and over for several minutes, then declares, "OK, time for bed."

That's it.

Sounds kinda dumb, I suppose. But to Tara? It is absolutely delightful. Before you judge that which she delights in, let me ask you something: What do you delight in? Perhaps you (or someone you love) delight in watching grown men running back and forth and putting a leather ball through a net, or maybe you like to see them carry a pigskin-covered oblong-shaped ball over a white line. Seems pretty dumb to me. Does that make it any less delightful to you? Probably not.

Maybe you delight in getting 50 percent off on a purchase. I know I do. Nothing can bring a smile to my face quicker than a smokin' deal! My opening line after a delightful day of shopping is always, "Honey, you won't believe how much money I *saved!*" Of course, my husband is quick to point out that Americans are the only people in the world who claim to save money by spending it.

Maybe you delight in making your home beautiful. Maybe you delight in making *yourself* beautiful. Some people delight in new cars, others in bragging about their kids' report cards. Some delight in traveling, cruising to exotic places; others delight in staying put on the couch, cruising with their remote control.

Nothing wrong with earthly delights, provided you don't become enslaved to them. However, just a moment ago the words to an old song popped into my head: *"Looking for love in all the wrong places . . ."* I suspect some of us have been looking for delight in all the wrong places. You can tell a lot about a person by the things he or she takes delight in.

The Bible says we should delight ourselves in *God.* And it tells us that *if* we delight ourselves in God, *then* he will give us the desires of our heart. Now wait a minute here. Does that mean that if I delight myself in God, he'll give me season tickets to see the Dallas Cowboys? If I delight myself in God, will he give me an unlimited clothing budget, heal me of all my diseases, and straighten out my finances? Some might interpret it that way.

However, I think when the Bible speaks of our *heart,* it is referring to the deepest place. That place that new clothes and new cars can never satisfy. The place that can be satisfied with nothing less than God himself. When we delight ourselves in God, the result is that he fills us with a knowledge of him and an unquenchable sense of his presence and glory.

I checked my dictionary and discovered that delight is another word for joy. Some weeks ago, my children, along with a neighbor boy, William, who attends our homeschool, were memorizing 1 Thessalonians 5:16–18: "Be joyful always; pray continually; give thanks in all circumstances, for this is God's will for you in Christ Jesus."

I can't resist a quick aside: The Bible is very new to William, and he's taking great delight in learning about God. One day I was standing in the kitchen, and William shouted, "Donna, you won't believe this!" I couldn't imagine what he was so astonished about. "What? What won't I believe?" I asked, giving him my full attention. "Well, one day this little boy, who was probably only MY age, went to Jesus and gave him five loaves of bread and two fish. And Jesus used it to feed 5,000 people!" He literally jumped out of his seat when he asked, "Can you believe that?" "That is definitely amazing," I said, unable to resist his excitement.

So back to this joy thing: One day my daughter Leah was fussing and fretting about something or another. (I can't imagine where she gets it; her *mother* never fusses or frets.) William turned to her and said very calmly, "Be joyful always. Pray continually."

He had hit the solution right on the head. I've heard it said that there are two surefire signs that we are guilty of practical atheism: lack of prayer and lack of joy. Think about that for a minute. Atheists don't pray to God because they don't believe he exists and, therefore, can't possibly answer. So what's our excuse? When we fail to pray, we are demonstrating in a very potent way what we really believe about God. True, we may believe he is there, but we obviously don't believe in his ability to answer prayer. A god who can't answer prayer isn't much of a god.

What of the lack of joy? Joylessness (could I have just invented a word?) is a rejection of our circumstances and, therefore, a rejection of the One who rules over our circumstances. If we believe that God is in control—that he is good and that he cares for us—we can have joy in the midst of any circumstance.

If we have that true joy, the joy of delighting in God's presence, we will be in prayer. And if we are praying continually, we will have joy. The two are intricately intertwined.

My daughter delights in my husband's nightly ritual, and she won't sleep without it. If we delight in God, we should have a nightly ritual with our heavenly Father—praying to him and delighting in his presence. Don't go to sleep without it!

Reflections Along the Journey

1. What do you delight in?

2. What can people learn about who you really are by observing the things you delight in?

3. In what ways have you been guilty of practical atheism (that is, lack of prayer or lack of joy)?

4. Don't be guilty of practical atheism—write out a prayer!

5. What key lesson did you glean from today's study?

Freedom Truths:

- You can tell a lot about a person by the things he or she takes delight in.
- Delight yourself in the Lord, and he will give you the desires of your heart.

Day Two

Delight in the God Who Rules

God reigns over the nations;
God is seated on his holy throne.

Psalm 47:8

Maybe it's because I became a Christian through the ministry of the Presbyterian Church, a denomination that's very big on the sovereignty of God; for whatever reason, I have always found tremendous comfort in the realization that God rules the universe. Benjamin Franklin put it this way: God governs over the affairs of men.

Does that make me fatalistic? Far from it! It infuses me with joy and confidence. I know there's nothing that can happen in my life—no decision I can make, no harm that can befall me—that can thwart God's ultimate purposes for my life. The psalmist wrote, "The Lord reigns, let the earth be *glad* [emphasis added]" (Psalm 97:1). The fact that God reigns is something we should be very glad about; it's good news.

Isn't it marvelous to know that God's purposes *will* stand? Indeed, they *must* stand. It is the very nature of his character to rule, the very definition of his sovereignty to be in control of all things, at all times. It's not just what he does; it's who he *is*. Although I'm far from advocating an obsession with doctrine for doctrine's sake, theology *does matter*. Our conception of God impacts our daily lives. It shapes everything we do, how we approach life, how we react to our circumstances.

With our loss of the sense of majesty has come the further loss of religious awe and consciousness of the divine Presence. We have lost our spirit of worship and our ability to withdraw inwardly to meet God in adoring silence. It is impossible to keep

166

our moral practices sound and our inward attitudes right while our idea of God is erroneous or inadequate. If we would bring back spiritual power to our lives, we must begin to think of God more nearly as He is.[1]

Set aside any preconceived notions you may have about the exaltation of man's "free will" (a phrase that does not appear *anywhere* in the entire Bible; I just checked both the *New International Version* and the King James Version), and truly study God's Word on this subject.

Just to get you started, ponder these passages:

The Lord reigns forever;
    he has established his throne for judgment.
He will judge the world in righteousness;
    he will govern the peoples with justice.
The Lord is a refuge for the oppressed,
    a stronghold in times of trouble.
Those who know your name will trust in you,
    for you, Lord, have never forsaken those who seek you.
(Psalm 9:7–10)

The Lord reigns, he is robed in majesty;
    the Lord is robed in majesty
    and is armed with strength.
The world is firmly established;
    it cannot be moved.
(Psalm 93:1)

Then I heard what sounded like a great multitude, like the roar of rushing waters and like loud peals of thunder, shouting: "Hallelujah! For our Lord God Almighty reigns. Let us rejoice and be glad and give him glory!" (Revelation 19:6–7).

Next, study the panorama of history. Again you will see the hand of God always moving mankind forward in accordance with his perfect will. For this purpose, I would highly recommend Diana Waring's marvelous cassette series "What in the World's Going on Here? Vol-

---

[1]Tozer, vii.

umes I and II."[2] If you thought history was boring, get these tapes. This woman *absolutely delights* in telling his story (history is his story) and I guarantee you will find her enthusiasm irresistible.

Don't get me wrong. I am not saying humans are mere puppets, that we have no choices to make. A. W. Tozer gives a wonderful illustration of this concept:

> An ocean liner leaves New York bound for Liverpool. Its destination has been determined by the proper authorities. Nothing can change it. On board the liner are several scores of passengers. They are not in chains, neither are their activities determined for them by decree. They are completely free to move about as they will. They eat, sleep, play, lounge about on the deck, read, talk, altogether as they please; but all the while the great liner is carrying them steadily onward toward a predetermined port. Both freedom and sovereignty are present here and they do not contradict each other. So it is, I believe, with man's freedom and the sovereignty of God. The mighty liner of God's sovereign design keeps its steady course over the sea of history. God moves undisturbed and unhindered toward the fulfillment of those eternal purposes which He purposed in Christ Jesus before the world began.[3]

God's purposes *will stand*. The only question is, where will *you* stand?

Reflections Along the Journey

1. Do you take delight in the knowledge that God rules the universe?

---

[2]To order, contact Diana Waring, 122 W. Grant, Spearfish, SD 57783 Phone: (605) 642–7583 www.dianawaring.com.
[3]Tozer, 111–12.

2. How can understanding God's sovereignty increase your joy and confidence?

3. Write out a prayer of praise to the God who rules the universe.

4. What key lesson did you glean from today's study?

Freedom Truths:

- Realizing that God rules should infuse us with joy and confidence.
- God's purposes will stand; the only question is, where will you stand?

Day Three

Delight Yourself in God's Word

But his delight is in the law of the Lord,
and on his law he meditates day and night.

Psalm 1:1

If you truly want to delight yourself in the God who rules, then you must delight yourself in his Word. For it is there that you see him personally intervening in the lives of his people. It is there that you see his character revealed: not only his sovereignty but his mercy and goodness, his holiness and justice, even his wrath and intolerance of all that is evil.

The simple truth is, "Your spiritual life will largely depend upon whether you learn to deal wisely and handle carefully God's Word."[4] Here's a passage that every Christian should memorize, because it holds forth a glorious promise for those who will take God's Word seriously:

Blessed is the man
    who does not walk in the counsel of the wicked
or stand in the way of sinners
    or sit in the seat of mockers.
But his delight is in the law of the Lord,
    and on his law he meditates day and night.
He is like a tree planted by streams of water,
    which yields its fruit in season
and whose leaf does not wither.
    Whatever he does prospers.
(Psalm 1:1–3)

---

[4]Andrew Murray, *The Believer's New Life* (Minneapolis, Minn.: Bethany House Publishers, 1984), 18.

Do you know what I find fascinating about this? When the psalmist writes that he delights in the "law of the Lord," he's talking about Leviticus and Deuteronomy. He's talking about the part of the Bible that some of us have never even read all the way through because we were so befuddled or bored to tears. (I'm just being honest!) When he says he was meditating day and night, he wasn't reading great stuff like the Psalms or the Prophets, certainly nothing as exciting as the Gospels or the book of Acts. How can you delight in stuff like "Build an altar of acacia wood, three cubits high; it is to be square, five cubits long and five cubits wide" (Exodus 27:1)? I mean, that just doesn't inspire me in the least. And yet the psalmist meditated on such words *because* they were the Word of God.

How fortunate we are to have all of God's Word to meditate on: all the beautiful poetry, the fascinating history, the practical letters. How much more quickly should we be able to declare:

> I meditate on your precepts
>   and consider your ways.
> I delight in your decrees;
>   I will not neglect your word.
> Your statutes are my delight;
>   they are my counselors.
> Direct me in the path of your commands,
>   for there I find delight.
> Turn my heart toward your statutes
>   and not toward selfish gain.
> Turn my eyes away from worthless things;
>   preserve my life according to your word.
> May your unfailing love be my comfort,
>   according to your promise to your servant.
> Let your compassion come to me that I may live,
>   for your law is my delight.
> (Psalm 119:15–16, 24, 35–37, 76–77)

I can't resist some more good stuff from Psalm 119:

> How can a young man keep his way pure?
>   By living according to your word.
> I seek you with all my heart;
>   do not let me stray from your commands.
> I have hidden your word in my heart

that I might not sin against you.
Praise be to you, O Lord;
   teach me your decrees.
With my lips I recount
   all the laws that come from your mouth.
I rejoice in following your statutes
   as one rejoices in great riches.
(Psalm 119:9–14)

OK, rock bottom: What does it mean to delight in God's Word? You know by now I'm not legalistic, but I'm gonna lay down one law: You need to read the Bible through every year. Don't even try to tell me it's too boring or too difficult. We just saw that the psalmist was able to take delight in the least fascinating portion of the Bible. We've got no excuse.

If you tell me you don't have time, I'll just have to jump off the page and smack you! The average American watches four hours of TV every day. Let's say you're well below average: you only watch the news for an hour. Let me save you some time: a house burned down, some guy crashed his car into a fire hydrant, a teenager shot at his _____ (teacher, mom, stepbrother, you fill in the blank). OK, now you know what's on the local news every night. Let me recap the national news: the politicians are crooked, and the world's falling apart at the seams, except for the beautiful people who are working hard to save the planet and rescue various insects from extinction. OK, now you know all about the national news.

I've just saved you an hour a day. See how good I am to you? Now invest that hour per day delighting in God's Word. I guarantee you'll read through it in a year, no problem.

One great option is the *One-Year Bible*, which provides a daily reading in the Old Testament, the New Testament, and the Psalms and Proverbs. In her latest book, *You've Got What It Takes* (Bethany House, 2000), my good friend and mentor Marita Littauer recommends *The Narrated Bible*, which is the *New International Version* arranged in chronological order, with historical narration provided by scholar F. LaGard Smith. I took her up on the suggestion and am thoroughly enjoying it. It does a marvelous job of making sense of Bible history. Now I know that the events of 1 Chronicles were the last to take place before the intertestamental period. And I bet you thought it was the stuff Malachi wrote about!

I don't usually use guilt as a motivator, but desperate times call for desperate measures. (I know we're in desperate times because most college graduates can't even recite the Ten Commandments.) Here comes the guilt trip: my nine-year-old daughter, Leah, has read through nine (count 'em, nine) Bibles in the last two years. You might protest, "Yeah, but those were just children's Bibles," to which I respond, "Yeah, but she's just a child." Besides, most of the Bibles were three hundred pages or more. *So there!* (I'm being a real brat today.)

Now for the clincher: Three months ago Leah came to me and said, "I'm sick of reading kids' Bibles. I want a REAL Bible." So off we went to the local Christian bookstore (where my teenager works, by the way). Leah picked out her very own Bible: the real thing, same edition any adult would read. While she slept, I tore out the entire Song of Solomon and various portions of the book of Judges. When she awoke the next morning, she began reading through her Bible at the rate of five chapters each weekday. As far as I know, she hasn't missed a day. She's currently reading through the book of Job.

So how far are YOU in your read-through-the-Bible-in-a-year program? Come on, you know you said you were gonna do it *this year*!

I'm heartily ashamed of myself for heaping all this shame upon you. But, hey, did it work???

Reflections Along the Journey

1. Have you been taking delight in God's Word? Why or why not?

2. Did my nine-year-old daughter Leah's delight in God's Word put you to shame or what?

3. What specific plan will you commit to for reading through the Bible in a year?

4. Write out a prayer committing to read through the Bible in a year.

5. What key lesson did you glean from today's study?

Freedom Truths:

- To delight in God's Word, we must read through it at least once a year.
- If the psalmist could delight in Leviticus, surely we can delight in the Psalms.

Day Four

Delight in the God Who Is Worthy to Be Praised

Great are the works of the Lord;
they are pondered by all who delight in them.

Psalm 111:2

If you've spent any time at all meditating upon the Psalms, you know they are filled with praise—praise for who God is, praise for what he has done and what he has promised to do. Psalm 111 provides a beautiful example of someone (the author is unknown) taking delight in God:

Praise the Lord.
I will extol the Lord with all my heart
    in the council of the upright and in the assembly.
Great are the works of the Lord;
    they are pondered by all who delight in them.
Glorious and majestic are his deeds,
    and his righteousness endures forever.
He has caused his wonders to be remembered;
    the Lord is gracious and compassionate.
He provides food for those who fear him;
    he remembers his covenant forever.
He has shown his people the power of his works,
    giving them the lands of other nations.
The works of his hands are faithful and just;
    all his precepts are trustworthy.
They are steadfast for ever and ever,
    done in faithfulness and uprightness.
He provided redemption for his people;
    he ordained his covenant forever—
    holy and awesome is his name.

The fear of the Lord is the beginning of wisdom;
   all who follow his precepts have good understanding.
   To him belongs eternal praise.

Read through this psalm again, marking all the praiseworthy actions and attributes of God. Go ahead! I'll wait for you.

The first thing I notice is the psalmist's "Well, duh" statement. He says that the Lord's great works "are pondered by all who delight in them." Translation: Well, duh! Of course we spend time thinking about what we delight in: whether it's a hobby, a sport, our children, or Pepperidge Farm Milano cookies. Our mind automatically drifts toward such thoughts. I think God deliberately designed our minds in such a way that once we know the delightful truth about who God is and all that he has done for us, we automatically think about such things. The trick, of course, is grabbing hold of the truths in the first place; our minds will take it from there.

So my challenge for you today is to fill your mind with delightful truths about God, starting with this psalm. Could you memorize it? Surely you could rewrite it and tape it up over your kitchen sink or next to your computer. But don't stop there. Why not set aside time to read through the entire book of Psalms? For an extra blessing, read them aloud.

Here's a little aside: If you have a job you can't handle and you don't think God can handle it either (whether it's a job inside or outside the home), try this: On the way to work (either in the car or in your bathroom before heading out to the breakfast table), listen to the Psalms being read aloud.

There are a couple of ways you can do this. You can buy the complete Bible on tape. I recently purchased *The Dramatized Holy Bible* (NIV) for well under $100. Some may consider that a bit pricey, but it's well worth the investment, especially for people who spend long hours in the car. Many church libraries have the Bible on tape, so before you buy, give that a try. Another option, if you are completing this study as part of a group, is to pitch in together to buy the Bible on tape, then keep the tapes circulating. Instant accountability: "So you were listening to 2 Peter this week? What did you learn?" Now, the other option: Read the Psalms aloud into a tape recorder, then you'll hear your own voice proclaiming the praiseworthy acts and attributes of God. Pretty powerful, don't you think?

You might make copies of the tapes and play them for your children. Don't you think it would have a tremendous influence on their little hearts and minds to hear their own mother or father extolling the greatness of God? The very next psalm, 112, assures us that this will be the case: "Blessed is the man who fears the Lord, who finds great delight in his commands. His *children* [emphasis added] will be mighty in the land" (Psalm 112:1b–2a).

Now that's a delightful promise if ever I've heard one! So if you want your children to be mighty in the land, what should you do? Move to a neighborhood with great schools? Enroll them in a private school? Buy them all the latest educational software? Keep them busy in sports so they learn leadership skills? How about piano lessons, voice lessons, gymnastics classes? The Bible says you should delight yourself in God's commands, then your "children will be mighty in the land."

Reflections Along the Journey

1. What steps can you take to fill your mind with the delightful acts and attributes of God?

2. What do you think is the connection between "taking delight in God's commands" and having "children [who] will be mighty in the land"?

3. What key lesson did you glean from today's study?

Freedom Truths:

- Our mind automatically drifts toward whatever we take delight in.
- If we delight in God's commands, our children will be mighty in the land.

Day Five

Delight in the God Who Delights in You

In love he predestined us to be adopted as his sons through Jesus Christ, in accordance with his pleasure and will—to the praise of his glorious grace, which he has freely given us in the One he loves.
Ephesians 1:4–6

If I have a claim to fame, and I'm not sure I do, it's probably my PWA teaching. For an in-depth understanding of PWA, you'll have to read *Walking in Total God-Confidence*. In a nutshell, the teaching is based on 1 John 3:1: "How great is the love the Father has lavished on us, that we should be called children of God! And that is what we are!"

Of course, you have to read the last sentence *with an attitude* or it doesn't work. It's something like this: You put your hands on your hips and swagger a bit as you shout with tremendous confidence, "And THAT is what we ARE. HUH!" You have to do this whole thing with a "So there!" tone of voice. We call that PWA: Princess WITH AN ATTITUDE.

By the way, it doesn't hurt to have a ridiculous looking tiara on your head. You can make your own out of aluminum foil. I know you people probably think I make this stuff up, but *just last night* I saw two women strutting around Wal-Mart with plastic tiaras on their heads. I was tempted to ask them if they had read my book.

Think about it: God is the King of the universe, the Creator and sustainer of all things. It's not like he needs a bunch of kids to make his life complete. Yet the Bible clearly teaches that he chose to adopt us. Us! A bunch of misfits! Just like Daddy Warbucks adopted Annie and showered her with wonderful gifts. Did he *need* a redheaded misfit? No way! So why complicate his life? Why bother? One very simple reason: because he *delighted* in her. (If you don't believe me, rent the movie *Annie*. Better yet, go see a live performance.)

In the same way, God chose to adopt us and shower us with wonderful gifts. Not because he needed us, but because he takes delight in us:

> Praise be to the God and Father of our Lord Jesus Christ, who has blessed us in the heavenly realms with every spiritual blessing in Christ. For he chose us in him before the creation of the world to be holy and blameless in his sight. In love he predestined us to be adopted as his sons through Jesus Christ, in accordance with his pleasure and will—to the praise of his glorious grace, which he has freely given us in the One he loves. (Ephesians 1:3–6)

The Bible is clear: God delights in his people! Who'd 'a thunk it? I sure wouldn't have. I mean, most of the Christians I know (including the one in the mirror) are a bunch of stumblebums. Do you ever feel like God is just *putting up with us*? You know you have those days with your own kids, right? Those days (weeks? months? years?) when they are far from a delight—you're just putting up with them 'cause they're yours and you wouldn't feel right about selling them to the gypsies.

God is *not* just putting up with us! He *delights* in us "as a bridegroom rejoices over his bride, so will your God rejoice over you" (Isaiah 62:5). Here's another one (so you know I'm not making this stuff up!): "The Lord delights in those who fear him, who put their hope in his unfailing love" (Psalm 147:11). Now here's a promise from the God who delights in you: "If the Lord delights in a man's way, he makes his steps firm; though he stumble, he will not fall, for the Lord upholds him with his hand" (Psalm 37:23–24).

Some time ago I received the following poem (I'm not sure what else to call it) in the mail. I share it with you in the hope that it will increase your delight in God:

CHOSEN FOR ROYALTY

I was chosen before the foundation of the world. (Eph. 1:4)
Chosen to be adopted into the family of God. (Gal. 3:26)
Before I was born, my inward parts were carefully formed.
(Ps. 139)

I was created in the image of God. (Gen. 1:26)
I am His special work of art. (Eph. 2:10)
Since God is my Abba Father (Rom. 8:15; Gal. 4:6)
And He is King of Kings, (Rev. 19:16)
I am a princess. (1 John 3:1)
Someday I will reign with Him. (Rev. 20:6)
I am a co-heir with Jesus. (Rom. 8:17)
I have an inheritance that nothing can destroy,
Reserved for me in heaven. (1 Pet. 1:4)
I am the cherished beloved one, (1 Thess. 1:4)
The spotless bride of Christ (Rev. 21:9)
On whom he has lavished His gifts of grace. (Eph. 1:8)
God did not spare His own Son for me.
Yes, he bought me with a price. (1 Cor. 6:20)
Not with silver or gold,
But with the precious blood of the Lamb. (1 Pet. 1:19)
Will He not freely give me all things? (Rom. 8:32)
Christ calls me His friend. (John 15:15)
We are so close that I am one with Him in Spirit. (1 Cor. 6:17)
I am whole, yes, complete in Him. (Col 2:10)
This body of mine is a sacred temple,
The temple of the Holy Spirit. (1 Cor. 6:19)
I am a holy saint, pure and blameless in God's sight (1 Cor. 1:2)
Because I am clothed with the righteousness of Christ.
    (2 Cor. 5:21)
Though many accuse and criticize me,
Jesus is my advocate who intercedes for me. (Rom. 8:34)
Though many may reject me,
I am accepted in the Beloved. (Eph. 1:6)
This is love, not that we loved God,
but that He loved us (1 John 4:9–19)
And chose us for His own. (John 15:17)

—Donna Fedukowski

Isn't that wonderfully encouraging? I haven't memorized it yet, but it's definitely on my list of "things to do." Why not add it to yours? When we meet someday, perhaps we'll recite it together. Just don't ask me to cite the references; I'm only human! (See, I'm letting you hold me accountable here. Kinda scary, if you want to know the truth.)

By now, I hope you are convinced that your Father delights in you. Delight yourself in him.

Reflections Along the Journey

1. What is the significance to your life of the statement: "You were chosen for royalty"?

2. As a first step toward memorizing "Chosen for Royalty," write it below in its entirety.

3. Write out a prayer expressing your delight in God.

4. What key lesson did you glean from today's study?

5. Write out this week's verse from memory.

Freedom Truths:

- We were chosen for royalty, adopted by the King.
- God delights in you, so delight yourself in him.

Weekly Review

See if you can fill in the seven steps toward living in absolute freedom. Look in the back of the book if you need help.

F _____ your bondage

R _____ your Deliverer

E _____ your liberty

E _____ your fellow slaves

D _____ yourself in God

O _____ pockets of resistance

M _____ forward in absolute freedom

WEEK NINE:
Overcome Pockets of Resistance

This Week's Verse:

Hear me, you who know what is right,
you people who have my law in your hearts:
Do not fear the reproach of men
or be terrified by their insults. . . .
I, even I, am he who comforts you.
Who are you that you fear mortal men?

Isaiah 51:7, 12

Day One

Higher Ground

From the ends of the earth I call to you,
I call as my heart grows faint;
lead me to the rock that is higher than I.

Psalm 61:2

I'd love for you to meet my pigmy goats, Mark and Luke. Now, a lot of people think they're just dumb, stubborn animals. Well, come to think of it, I guess they are. They aren't particularly useful, either. I can't milk them (they're both males, as you may have guessed by the names). I wouldn't dream of slaughtering them for their meat. They can't bark if a prowler shows up on the premises. They eat everything in sight . . . especially my husband's precious rosebushes. My husband cannot for the life of him figure out what I see in these goats. He says they're useless, and when I think about it rationally I must admit he's right.

But I don't care. I love them to pieces anyway. I call them my babies, and I enjoy spending time with them. My favorite time of day is our morning climb. I wake up, usually to the sound of our roosters crowing, and head out to the goat pen. I feed the chickens and ducks, water my garden, and then it's climb time. I let the goats out and start leading the way to the mountaintop. Each day I hope against hope that *this* is the day we can climb without resistance, without delays or detours. Those days are rare indeed.

You see, the house next door is under construction. And like most construction sites, it's an eternal mess: Styrofoam coffee cups, fast-food restaurant wrappings, wood scraps, nails. You get the picture. For some inexplicable reason, my goats find this trash heap irresistibly appealing. They'd rather wallow in the mess than follow me to higher ground.

Sometimes all I have to do is coax them back onto the path. Sometimes I bribe them with their favorite honey-and-grain mix (their candy bars, if you will). Some days I actually pick them up. Then there are days when I have to take a tree limb and do some serious persuasion.

As you can imagine, the workmen think I'm a lunatic. I'm sure they wonder, *Why on earth does she bother with those dumb animals? Why doesn't just she leave them alone and let them enjoy the trash heap?*

Good questions.

It's because I know something the workmen don't know. I know that despite all their protests, once I take my goats to the mountain-top—even as we begin the ascent to higher ground—they remember: *This is what we were created to do.* And when we get to the top of that mountain, as I sit on my prayer rock overlooking the valley, the goats are filled with joy. They leap from rock to rock, then come snuggling up to me, as if to say, *How can we thank you enough for reminding us who we really are?*

We are never so close as we are on the mountaintop. It is only there that they lay at my feet, content. When I see their joy and con-tentment, I know that the battle was worth it. And I tell myself, "Eventually, they'll catch on. They'll come with me willingly." Some-times they come without resistance; often they don't.

One day as I sat on my rock thinking, I realized, *I'm just like those goats!* God wants to take me to higher ground. He wants to take me to the place where I can see life from his perspective, but I resist him. I fight him tooth and nail. Even though I know the joy and tranquility I experience when I climb the mountain to fellowship with God, how many days do I ignore his call? How many days do I stay in bed? How often do I prefer the trash heap to the mountaintop?

I guess I'm as dumb as those goats. Often I'm just as useless. Yet God loves me and longs to fellowship with me, just as he longs to fellowship with you. God is calling us to higher ground. Will we re-sist? Or will we follow willingly?

Reflections Along the Journey

1. In what ways have you sensed God calling you to higher ground?

2. Is there a specific place you have set aside to meet with God? If not, arrange one. It might be a place outdoors, in your neighborhood, or in your home. Where will you plan to meet with God?

3. In what ways have you resisted God's called to higher ground?

4. What are some practical ways you might become less resistant?

5. Write out a prayer of commitment to follow God to higher ground.

6. What key lesson did you glean from today's study?

Freedom Truths:

- God is calling us to higher ground. We can choose to resist or to respond.
- God wants to take us to a place where we can see life from his perspective.

Day Two

Overcoming Doubt

If any of you lacks wisdom, he should ask God, who gives generously to all without finding fault, and it will be given to him. But when he asks, he must believe and not doubt, because he who doubts is like a wave of the sea, blown and tossed by the wind. That man should not think he will receive anything from the Lord; he is a double-minded man, unstable in all he does.

James 1:5–8

It had been a couple of years since I last visited the Christian bookstore in Scottsdale, Arizona. Our family had moved a couple hours north to the mountains, but I had been to that bookstore so many times, I was confident I could still remember the way. A friend had given me a gift certificate—enough to buy the Bible on audiocassette—and I was so excited I thought I would burst.

I pulled off the freeway and headed south on the road I was confident would lead me to the bookstore. Five minutes turned into ten minutes. Ten minutes turned into fifteen minutes. "Hmmm. I don't remember it being this far south. Maybe I passed it. No, wait a minute. I know it's farther than OfficeMax." Five more minutes. I began slowing down at every intersection, peering into every shopping center. The drivers behind me were not happy. "Wait. I remember this. OK. Yeah, it's the next street." Except it wasn't the next street.

After about twenty minutes of this dialogue with myself, I threw up my hands in frustration. "How could I be such an idiot? How could I get lost going to the Christian bookstore? I must have passed it long ago!" I made an illegal U-turn and headed north, slowing down at every intersection, growing more exasperated with each passing minute. So much for my joyous expedition.

Another twenty minutes passed. Finally, in complete resignation,

I pulled into a parking lot and asked the first guy I saw if he knew where the intersection of Roosevelt and Hayden was. He didn't, but amazingly enough he had a map and, unlike most men, was willing to look at it. Aha! There it was—about twenty minutes south.

I hopped back into my car, heading south. Confident. This time I knew for sure where I was going. When I got to the intersection where I had made the illegal U-turn, I looked up—and saw the roof of the Christian bookstore. I almost smacked myself! After two hours of driving, I had given up just two minutes from my destination. I had been on the right path all along, I just didn't believe it. As a result, I ended up wasting an hour of time and probably lost a year off my life.

I think I do that a lot. Second-guessing myself. Slowing down when I should be going full-speed ahead. Backtracking when I should be moving forward. God gives me clear direction and I set out to where I know he is leading me. Confident. Then, just when I'm almost there, I'm plagued with doubt. I turn back. I waste time and drive myself—and everyone around me—to distraction.

It happened to me just this year. God clearly gave me a new direction for my life, and I began pursuing it with enthusiasm. God did everything but come down and tell me face-to-face that I was on the right path. And just when I had almost made it through to my destination, I became plagued by doubt. *Did God really say what I thought he said? Maybe I'm lost and I don't even know it!* As a result, I gave up, turned back, and will have to travel a painful road all over again.

It's possible to be on the right path but be so plagued by doubt that you're no better off than someone who is completely lost. God is not interested in keeping secrets from you. He hasn't sent you on a scavenger hunt. The Bible tells us that if any of us lacks wisdom—lacks direction for our life—we should ask God, and he will gladly give it to us (James 1:5). But when God answers, we must believe him. Then we must act on that belief, always moving forward in faith.

Stop making U-turns! Look up and see your final destination!

Reflections Along the Journey

1. Can you think of a time when you were so plagued by doubt, you were no better off than someone who was completely lost?

2. Have you ever made a U-turn in your life, only to realize later that you had been on the right path all along?

3. What were the consequences of making a U-turn when you should have been moving forward in faith?

4. Write out a prayer asking God for confidence to move forward in faith.

5. What key lesson did you glean from today's study?

Freedom Truths:

- It is possible to be on the right path but be so plagued by doubt that you're no better off than someone who is completely lost.
- Stop making U-turns and move forward in faith.

Day Three

Overcoming Conflicting Desires

> What causes fights and quarrels among you? Don't they come from your desires that battle within you?
>
> James 4:1

I long to be a great mom, but I think I deserve a break today.

I long to have a great marriage, but I want Prince Charming to come rescue me.

I long to make an eternal difference, but I want to look good and enjoy the creature comforts of this world.

I long to renew my mind, but I want to kick back and watch TV.

I long to know God's Word, but I also want to daydream, to indulge my fantasies.

I long for a peaceful home, but I want my own way *now*.

I long to take care of my temple, my body, but I want to please my tastebuds, to savor foods I know are destructive to my body.

I long to live a godly life, but sometimes I want to get away with something, to take the easy way out.

As I reflect on why I haven't made greater progress in my spiritual walk, I realize it's not that I don't desire to lead a godly life. I fervently do. I couldn't figure out what kept throwing me off in my journey toward living in absolute freedom. I would cry out, *Lord, you know I want to be a godly woman, a woman of prayer, an amazing mother. You know how I long for these things, so why don't you grant them to me?*

That's when God showed me a pocket of resistance big enough to hold a continent: *other desires*. I have other desires that conflict with my righteous desires. And to the extent that those other desires take precedence, I will continue with my two-steps-forward, three-steps-back routine. I failed to realize that there is an internal war waging in the area of my desires. I can't imagine why I didn't know it, because the Bible clearly spells it out: "What causes fights and quarrels among you? Don't they come from your desires that battle within you?"

I always thought of that verse in terms of church conflicts and disputes. I never thought about the war *within myself*. And yet when I think about it, I know just how real the war is. There is a war going on inside of you too. The question is, are you showing up for battle armed for victory, or are you just sitting back hoping everything will turn out all right? If you're going to win, you've got to aggressively ferret out those pockets of resistance in your heart.

I believe today's battle plan will be a tremendous step forward in that direction. I read about this concept in *The Mind of Christ*.[1] Here's my slightly modified version of their recommendations:

STEP ONE: Sit down with several sheets of blank paper and a pen. Make out a list of every desire you have, every desire that springs to mind. Don't screen them, just write them down. You might write something like:

I desire to:
> read through the Bible this year
> be a godly wife
> run away with Tom Cruise
> love my kids
> sell my kids to the gypsies
> sleep for ninety-eight hours

STEP TWO: Rewrite your list, dividing it into two columns: Positive Desires and DTOs (Desires to Overcome). Add a third column for Strategy—how you will work through these desires.

STEP THREE: Now take a colored marker and draw a line between desires that clearly conflict with each other. For example, running away with Tom Cruise would conflict with your desire to be a devoted wife. So link those two. Keep going through the list. Some DTOs may conflict with more than one "positive desire" and vice versa. That's OK; do the best you can to link them up in an organized fashion.

STEP FOUR: Prioritize your positive desires—which are the most

---

[1]T. W. Hunt and Claude V. King, *The Mind of Christ* (Nashville: Lifeway Press, 1994), 34.

important for you to pursue? If some of these desires are in conflict with more than one DTO, rank the DTOs in the order you'd like to overcome them.

STEP FIVE: Neatly transfer your list here. (For now, leave the strategy column blank. We'll get to that in a minute.)

STEP SIX: Go through the list row by row and put an asterisk next to the desire that is winning the battle, whether it be a positive one or a DTO.

STEP SEVEN: Underneath the Strategy column, for each DTO, list one action step you can take to actively battle against it. For example, your strategy to overcome your desire to run away with Tom Cruise might be: "Don't rent Tom Cruise movies." In my case, "Look in the mirror and THINK" would also work.

STEP EIGHT: Review your list daily, paying particular attention to the strategy column. If you are going to overcome the DTOs, you're gonna have to fight!

Well, that's it, folks. You've got the eight steps to freedom over pockets of resistance. The trick now is to implement them.

Positive Desires   **DTOs**   **Strategy**

Reflections Along the Journey

1. Were you surprised by how many conflicting desires you had? Describe your reaction.

2. Describe your reaction to today's exercise.

3. Write out a prayer asking God to help you overcome conflicting desires.

4. What key lesson did you glean from today's study?

Freedom Truths:

- Although we may have godly desires, we also have *other conflicting desires* that take precedence over our godly desires.
- These conflicting desires are at war with one another. The side on which we battle most vigorously will win.

Day Four

Overcoming the Fear of Man

Hear me, you who know what is right,
*   you people who have my law in your hearts:*
Do not fear the reproach of men
*   or be terrified by their insults. . . .*
I, even I, am he who comforts you.
Who are you that you fear mortal men?

Isaiah 51:7, 12

The lesson started with a letter. It was a letter from my daughter's tennis coach[2] lambasting her for being a lazy, irresponsible child and, by inference, blasting me for being a lazy, irresponsible mother. I was furious. I was indignant. For weeks my blood boiled.

Even though I didn't even like this woman and we were thinking about firing her anyway, I suddenly felt this overwhelming urge to justify myself in her eyes. I needed to prove to this woman—I needed to EXPLAIN to her—why she had misjudged us. I couldn't bear to think that someone was out there thinking ill of my child . . . and of me. In short, I feared her reproach and I was terrified of her insults.

So I sat down and wrote her a long letter. I spent hours crafting it, explaining step by step exactly how she had misunderstood and, therefore, misjudged our family. Well, I get paid good money to write good stuff, and by the time I was finished with my letter, I pronounced it good. In fact, I considered it an incredibly *nice letter* given the tone of the letter to which I was responding. I felt satisfied—*now she'd see that I was right. She'd change her mind about us and come groveling for forgiveness and reconciliation.* (This just goes to prove

---

[2]OK, so she doesn't really have a tennis coach, but if I tell you who the letter was *really* from, that would be gossip.

how neurotic I am, given that a week earlier I was planning to fire her.)

Unfortunately I failed to consider that she was battling the very same pocket of resistance I was. She, too, was overcome with an irresistible urge to justify *herself*, to prove *her case*, to prove that she was—and ever would remain—absolutely right. And furthermore, that I was—and ever would remain—absolutely wrong. Boy, what a letter I got in return! YIKES!

The thought of writing back crossed my mind, but I resisted. And ever since I have savored that triumph. Yes, it *was* possible to overcome the urge to justify myself and to instead let God be my Comforter.

The book of Proverbs warns us: "Fear of man will prove to be a snare, but whoever trusts in the Lord is kept safe" (Proverbs 29:25).

Jesus set an example for us to follow. He kept silent when men reproached him and hurled their insults at him. He didn't attempt to justify himself; he let the Father be his justifier. Yes, there is a time to speak, but more often, it's better to keep silent. Proverbs 19:11 says: "A man's wisdom gives him patience; it is to his glory to overlook an offense."

I know how hard this is! As I ponder the pockets of resistance in my own life, those areas of sin that seem impervious to all my prayers and New Year's resolutions, I realize that many of them are rooted in the fear of man. Time after time I get into trouble trying to prove that *I'm right* or, more commonly, that I've been misunderstood. I'd encourage you to consider how many of your resistant sins have the same root cause.

Do you realize that it is literally impossible to live your life in a way that will win everyone's approval? Now, that can become either a bondage or the most freeing truth you've ever heard. I hope it's the latter.

Having thought a great deal about this, I've come up with a sure-fire method to root out the fear of man: Stop explaining yourself. Here's the theory: since all explanations are rooted in the fear of man, all explanations are rooted in pride, aka sin. What do you think?

Why do we feel compelled to explain why we are late? Because we're afraid people will think less of us; we fear their reproach and their insults. An apology is in order, certainly. So is a determination to arrive on time *next time*. But an explanation? Unnecessary.

One of my pastimes is *explaining* my children's behavior to other people: "Well, she usually takes a nap around now . . ." If your child behaves badly, have him apologize, then take him home, discipline him, and train him better for the future. But an explanation? Ineffective.

Lately I've heard myself doing quite a bit of explaining about my weight. Do you think any of my listeners are genuinely interested in why I'm twenty pounds overweight? I doubt it. If I'm concerned about my weight, I should eat less and exercise more. It's that simple. But an explanation? Pathetic.

You get the idea! Try it. I think you'll come to the same conclusion about the inherent sinfulness of explanations. So if you ever catch me offering up explanations, you have my permission to reproach and insult me. It's OK. God says he'll comfort me.

Reflections Along the Journey

1. Can you think of areas of sin in your life (attitudes and actions) that are rooted in the fear of man?

2. What do you think of the idea that all explanations of personal behavior are rooted in the sin of pride?

3. Think of a recent occasion when you felt compelled to explain yourself. Examine your heart to discover whether or not you were motivated by a desire to justify yourself.

4. Write out a prayer asking God to set you free from the urge to explain.

5. What key lesson did you glean from today's study?

Freedom Truths:

- We try to justify ourselves and explain our actions because we fear the reproach of men.
- All explanations of personal behavior are rooted in the sin of pride.

Day Five

Overcoming the Power of Lies

Then you will know the truth, and the truth will set you free.
John 8:32

As I reviewed Days 1 through 4, pondering what profound spiritual insight to drop upon you for our final day of "Overcome Pockets of Resistance," it suddenly hit me: In every case, what we need to do is overcome lies.

Think about it for a minute. We don't follow God to higher ground—that is, we resist God's call to fellowship—because we're believing lies. We're believing that extra sleep will be more refreshing than getting out of bed to have time alone with God. The truth is nothing on earth can be more refreshing than *quality time* spent at the throne of grace. The Muslims have a saying: "Prayer is better than sleep." Although I could do without their false religion, they've got that truth nailed down. I often mumble, "Prayer is better than sleep" to myself at those moments when it seems nothing could possibly be better than sleep.

Overcome the lie with the truth. The truth kills lies.

We wander the streets, begging spiritual bread, looking for a new church, a new spiritual mentor, some new spiritual "experience," because we're believing lies. We're believing that we need God AND . . . something else, something more. The truth is God has given us everything we need for life and godliness. The truth is right there before our eyes, if we will just open them.

Overcome the lie with the truth. The truth kills lies.

We live enslaved to conflicting desires because we're believing lies. We're believing that those *other things* we're longing for can fulfill us. We're believing that those DTOs can do more for us than our

201

positive desires can, our righteous and holy desires. The truth is nothing can be more fulfilling than the pursuit of righteousness. Nothing can make us happier than becoming the person God is calling us to be.

Overcome the lie with the truth. The truth kills lies.

We live in fear of man because we think human opinion counts for something. It doesn't. It's a lie. God's opinion is the *only* one that counts. We have a slogan at our house: "We live our lives before an audience of One." The truth is God's opinion is the only one that counts.

Overcome the lie with the truth. The truth kills lies.

Let's do another class participation project here. Note some of the lies you have been believing, then note what truth from God's Word will enable you to overcome the lie. I've given you a few examples to get you going:

LIE	TRUTH
I'm worthless.	I'm a child of the King.
No one likes me.	God adores me.
I've been abandoned.	God will never leave me.
I can't overcome _____.	I can do all things through Christ who strengthens me.

Reflections Along the Journey

1. Have you been believing some lies? What are they?

2. What truths do you need to cling to in order to overcome those lies?

3. Write out a prayer rejecting lies and embracing truth.

4. What key lesson did you glean from today's study?

5. Write out this week's verse from memory.

Freedom Truths:

- We get into trouble when we believe lies about who we are or who God is.
- We can overcome lies with the truth. The truth kills lies.

Weekly Review

See if you can fill in the seven steps toward living in absolute freedom. Look in the back of the book if you need help.

F _____ your bondage

R _____ your Deliverer

E _____ your liberty

E _____ your fellow slaves

D _____ yourself in God

O _____ pockets of resistance

M _____ forward in absolute freedom

WEEK TEN:
Move Forward in Absolute Freedom

This Week's Verse:

Remember how the Lord your God led you all the way in the
desert these forty years, to humble you and to test you in order
to know what was in your heart, whether or not you
would keep his commands.

Deuteronomy 8:2

Day One

Set Free to Live Free

Remember how the Lord your God led you all the way in the desert these forty years, to humble you and to test you in order to know what was in your heart, whether or not you would keep his commands.

Deuteronomy 8:2

Let's begin this final week together by exploring an extended passage from God's Word. First, the background: The people of Israel had been delivered from the hands of the Egyptians some forty years earlier. They had been set free and were headed toward the Promised Land. Unfortunately, they didn't understand HOW TO LIVE AS FREE PEOPLE. Now as they stand on the brink of all that God has promised, Moses speaks to the assembled people. He reminds them of their history: how God has miraculously intervened, time and time again. He reminds them of how God had performed wonders on their behalf, how he delivered them with a mighty hand and an outstretched arm, how he sustained them in the desert. He explained the Ten Commandments to them. He warned them against turning back to Egypt in their hearts and against embracing the false gods of the people among whom they are about to live.

Now in Deuteronomy 8 he explains what it takes to *live in freedom*. The Israelites have learned the hard way that being set free is NOT the same as living in freedom. God set them free forty years ago, but they've wandered around enslaved by their own unbelief and foolish choices.

It's time to enter into their freedom. And so Moses is about to explain to them how having been set free they can begin to actually LIVE FREE. Since God has done a mighty work in our lives these past nine weeks, delivering us from bondage, it is well for us to heed

Moses' instructions on how we, too, can live free:

Be careful to follow every command I am giving you today, so that you may live and increase and may enter and possess the land that the Lord promised on oath to your forefathers. Remember how the Lord your God led you all the way in the desert these forty years, to humble you and to test you in order to know what was in your heart, whether or not you would keep his commands. He humbled you, causing you to hunger and then feeding you with manna, which neither you nor your fathers had known, to teach you that man does not live on bread alone but on every word that comes from the mouth of the Lord. Your clothes did not wear out and your feet did not swell during these forty years. Know then in your heart that as a man disciplines his son, so the Lord your God disciplines you.

Observe the commands of the Lord your God, walking in his ways and revering him. For the Lord your God is bringing you into a good land—a land with streams and pools of water, with springs flowing in the valleys and hills; a land with wheat and barley, vines and fig trees, pomegranates, olive oil and honey; a land where bread will not be scarce and you will lack nothing; a land where the rocks are iron and you can dig copper out of the hills.

When you have eaten and are satisfied, praise the Lord your God for the good land he has given you. Be careful that you do not forget the Lord your God, failing to observe his commands, his laws and his decrees that I am giving you this day. Otherwise, when you eat and are satisfied, when you build fine houses and settle down, and when your herds and flocks grow large and your silver and gold increase and all you have is multiplied, then your heart will become proud and you will forget the Lord your God, who brought you out of Egypt, out of the land of slavery. He led you through the vast and dreadful desert, that thirsty and water-less land, with its venomous snakes and scorpions. He brought you water out of hard rock. He gave you manna to eat in the desert, something your fathers had never known, to humble and to test you so that in the end it might go well with you. You may say to yourself, "My power and the strength of my hands have produced this wealth for me." But remember the Lord your God, for it is he who gives you the ability to produce wealth, and so confirms his covenant, which he swore to your forefathers, as it is today. (Deuteronomy 8:1–18)

Now carefully reread the passage, this time noting your insights concerning the following:

1. What do we need to be careful to do?

2. What do we need to remember?

3. Why did God allow the Israelites to wander around the desert, even after they had been set free?

4. What potential pitfalls does God warn them against?

5. What relevance does this passage have for your life?

Throughout the remainder of this week, we'll explore the answers to these questions together. Let me just say this: I find it tremendously comforting to know that God not only set his people free, he instructed them how to live in freedom. That's because former slaves who enter into freedom must learn a whole new way of living.

Reflections Along the Journey

1. Having been set free, how does God want us to live?

2. Recap any key insights you gained from your own personal study of today's passage.

3. Write out a prayer expressing your desire to live free.

4. What key lesson did you glean from today's study?

Freedom Truths:

- God not only sets us free, he instructs us how to live in freedom.
- When we enter into freedom, we need to learn a whole new way of living.

Day Two

Life in the Promised Land

Life in the Promised Land is *not* a carefree life; it is quite the contrary. God's Word says it requires great care to live in freedom. Indeed, we see a pattern throughout the Bible: obedience and freedom are linked, just as disobedience and slavery are linked. When the people of Israel obeyed God, they lived in peace; when they rebelled against him, they were invariably taken into captivity. Study the prophets and see how God warns his people, again and again: *I want you to remain free, THEREFORE, repent. If you don't repent, you'll end up in chains.*

It's amazing to me how we can breeze through portions of the Bible for years and then, all of a sudden, BAM! I remember earlier this year sitting in the Sacramento Airport for hours (long story), reading through Isaiah with such wonder and excitement it was as if I were reading it for the very first time. I highlighted these passages:

I took you from the ends of the earth,
    from its farthest corners I called you.
I said, "You are my servant";
    I have chosen you and have not rejected you.
So do not fear, for I am with you;
    do not be dismayed, for I am your God.
I will strengthen you and help you;
    I will uphold you with my righteous right hand.
All who rage against you
    will surely be ashamed and disgraced;
those who oppose you
    will be as nothing and perish.
Though you search for your enemies,
    you will not find them.
Those who wage war against you

will be as nothing at all.
For I am the Lord, your God,
    who takes hold of your right hand
and says to you, Do not fear;
    I will help you.
(Isaiah 41:9–13)

Since you are precious and honored in my sight,
    and because I love you,
I will give men in exchange for you,
    and people in exchange for your life.
Do not be afraid, for I am with you.
(Isaiah 43:4–5)

I am he, I am he who will sustain you.
    I have made you and I will carry you;
I will sustain you and I will rescue you.
(Isaiah 46:4)

As if those passages weren't awesome enough, here's the clincher: "See, I have engraved you on the palms of my hands" (Isaiah 49:16).

Have you ever read such beautiful, encouraging words? It wasn't until earlier this week that it occurred to me: *What is the* context *of Isaiah?* It is this: God is warning the people to repent. He is telling them that the only way to live in freedom is to live in obedience; if they persist in disobedience, they'll be enslaved. They refused to repent, and, sure enough, they were hauled away by the Babylonians.

Here we see God's love and holiness standing side by side. One does not mitigate the other; indeed, each makes the other possible. God loves us; he has engraved us on the palm of his hands; he created us to live in absolute freedom. NEVERTHELESS. Note that word: NEVERTHELESS, unless we learn *how to live in freedom*, that freedom will be taken from us. Does that sound harsh? No. It's just one of the immutable laws of the universe. Even our justice system reflects this basic truth: Those who can't handle their freedom eventually get locked behind bars. Granted, they may get away with abusing their freedoms for a season, but it eventually catches up with them.

God loves us, but that doesn't mean we can jump off a thirty-story building and expect him to suspend the laws of the universe. He won't. We're gonna crash. The same is true in the spiritual realm. God will not suspend the laws of the spiritual universe. We reap what we sow, forgiveness notwithstanding:

> Do not be deceived: God cannot be mocked. A man reaps what he sows. The one who sows to please his sinful nature, from that nature will reap destruction; the one who sows to please the Spirit, from the Spirit will reap eternal life. Let us not become weary in doing good, for at the proper time we will reap a harvest if we do not give up. (Galatians 6:7–9)

I found this interesting application of Deuteronomy 8 in the *NIV Life Application Bible*. We obey God with:

OUR HEART	by loving him more than any relationship, activity, achievement, or possession.
OUR WILL	by committing ourselves completely to him.
OUR MIND	by seeking to know him and his Word, so that his principles and values form the foundation of all we think and do.
OUR BODY	by recognizing that our strengths, talents, and sexuality are given to us by God to be used for pleasure and fulfillment according to his rules, not ours.
OUR FINANCES	by deciding that all of the resources we have ultimately come from God, and that we are to be managers of them and not owners.
OUR FUTURE	by deciding to make service to God and man the main purpose of our life's work.[1]

We have spent an entire day answering Question #1 from yesterday: *What do we need to be careful to do?* We need to be careful to live in obedience. Only then can we live in the freedom God has prepared for us.

---

[1]*The NIV Life Application Bible* (Grand Rapids, Mich.: Zondervan Publishing House, 1991), 293.

Reflections Along the Journey

1. What is the significance of this statement? Obedience and freedom are linked just as disobedience and slavery are linked.

2. How have you seen this "immutable law of the universe" at work in your own life?

3. Write out a prayer repenting of disobedience and expressing your desire to live in obedience.

4. What key lesson did you glean from today's study?

Freedom Truths:

- Obedience and freedom are linked just as disobedience and slavery are linked.
- We reap what we sow, forgiveness notwithstanding.

Day Three

Freedom Through Remembrance

These stones are to be a memorial to the people of Israel forever.
Joshua 4:7b

A small slip of paper tumbled out of my Bible earlier today. Written on it were my "Stones of Remembrance." I had recorded some of the most significant events in my Christian life. Only God knows the mighty miracles that were performed to make each of these Stones of Remembrance possible:

- Fifth Grade—Camp Lebanon (a Baptist youth camp in Pennsylvania). God gave me seeds of faith and a vision of a better future.
- March 1980—Heard and believed the gospel at Sandy Cove youth conference, although I did not begin to live as a Christian.
- July 1980—Received Christ as Savior and Lord at Tuscarora Conference Center. God told me, in a very personal way, that he would use my life to make a difference in this world. My spiritual pilgrimage began in earnest.
- 1980–1990—Wilderness wanderings.
- August 1990—God confirmed the call to writing. My first book contract with Focus on the Family.
- July 1993—Spiritual gifts class. Understood why I see the world the way I do; understood the nature of my call to ministry.
- December 1994—God revealed that I will have a twofold ministry: "Comforting the Afflicted and Afflicting the Comfortable."
- March 1996—Women of Virtue conference, Tuscon, AZ. God confirmed the call to speaking ministry.
- February 22, 1997—Franciscan Renewal Center, Scottsdale, AZ. God laid on my heart the outline for *Walking in Total God-Confidence*.

● November 4, 1998—Hotel room in Oklahoma City, OK. God laid on my heart the outline for this book, along with ideas for several more.

● New Year's Eve, 1999—God challenged me to do "smaller things with greater faithfulness."

I want to give you the opportunity today to think back upon your spiritual pilgrimage and set up Stones of Remembrance of your own, but first, let me show you the biblical basis for what we're about to do. Here's the scene: Moses has died, never to set foot in the Promised Land. Joshua has assumed command, and now, after four hundred years in slavery followed by forty years wandering in the wilderness, the people of Israel have finally entered into the land of freedom. But before they rush off into a whole new way of life, God says, STOP. THINK. REMEMBER.

> When the whole nation had finished crossing the Jordan, the Lord said to Joshua, "Choose twelve men from among the people, one from each tribe, and tell them to take up twelve stones from the middle of the Jordan from right where the priests stood and to carry them over with you and put them down at the place where you stay tonight."
> So Joshua called together the twelve men he had appointed from the Israelites, one from each tribe, and said to them, "Go over before the ark of the Lord your God into the middle of the Jordan. Each of you is to take up a stone on his shoulder, according to the number of the tribes of the Israelites, to serve as a sign among you. In the future, when your children ask you, 'What do these stones mean?' tell them that the flow of the Jordan was cut off before the ark of the covenant of the Lord. When it crossed the Jordan, the waters of the Jordan were cut off. These stones are to be a memorial to the people of Israel forever" (Joshua 4:1–7).

God wants us to REMEMBER. *What does God want us to remember?* (That was the second question we posed on Day 1; we'll get to the other two questions tomorrow.) He wants us to remember who he is, what he's done, and what he's capable of doing. That way, when we face obstacles in the Promised Land, as we surely will, our hearts won't faint. Our Stones of Remembrance are also to be a witness to our children that our faith is *real*.

Now I want you to set up Stones of Remembrance of your own. Stop. Think. Remember all that God has done for you: the times he has spoken clearly, the prayers he has answered, the miracles he has performed. It's my fervent prayer that this *Ten-Week Journey to Living in Absolute Freedom* will have been significant enough in your life that you will include it among your Stones of Remembrance. I know it's hard to think back and remember the details, but that's *exactly why* it's so important for you to take time to remember. Once you've written out your list, copy it into the front of your Bible so you can keep it up-to-date as God continues to work miracles in your life.

❧

❧

❧

❧

❧

❧

❧

❧

Reflections Along the Journey

1. What does God want us to remember?

2. Why does he want us to remember?

3. Recap one or two of your most significant Stones of Remembrance.

4. Write out a prayer of remembrance.

5. What key lesson did you glean from today's study?

Freedom Truths:

- God wants us to remember.
- Each of us needs to set up Stones of Remembrances along our spiritual journey.

Day Four

To Know What's in Your Heart

Remember how the Lord your God led you all the way in the desert these forty years, to humble you and to test you in order to know what was in your heart, whether or not you would keep his commands.

Deuteronomy 8:2

Along my spiritual pilgrimage, you may have noticed my ten years of "wilderness wanderings." Throughout most of the 1980s I was in a spiritual desert despite the fact that we hosted excellent small group Bible studies in our home. I also taught Sunday school, worked in youth ministry, baked casseroles, and planned fellowship activities—all the usual church stuff. Nevertheless, it was not a time of mighty miracles, answered prayers, or voices from heaven. It was a time of plodding forward.

That's part of the journey, too, you know: plodding. Sometimes it takes greater faith to plod through the silences than to "take a leap of faith" in response to God's call. Which brings us to Question #3 (posed back on Day 1): *Why did God allow the Israelites to wander around the desert, even after they had been set free?* The answer is found in our memory verse for this week and this day: "Remember how the Lord your God led you all the way in the desert these forty years, to humble you and to test you in order to know what was in your heart, whether or not you would keep his commands."

When God led the people into the desert, they expected something completely different from what they got. They expected to make an eleven-day journey to the Land of Milk and Honey. Put another way, they expected to be living on Easy Street with two cars in the garage and Pizza Hut for dinner every Friday night.

It didn't work out that way.

Has God ever led you to a place, and when you got there it was something completely different from what you expected? In 1992 God led me to leave behind everything I knew and move to Arizona. As I drove cross-country with my two-year-old daughter in the back-seat, we joyfully sang a children's song about God leading Abraham to a new land. What wonders would God perform? What mighty miracles were awaiting us? I felt certain that since God led us, surely his purpose was to bless us *immediately*. Right?

Instead, my husband endured five long years of unemployment and underemployment. Truth be told, I never did find a *single customer* for my marketing communications business, which had done quite well on the East Coast. Thankfully most of my East Coast customers continued to send me some work. Otherwise we literally would have starved. We inched toward bankruptcy. We plunged toward despair.

I remember walking under the streetlights one night shaking my fist in the air, asking God the same question the Israelites had posed thousands of years before, *"Did you bring us into this desert to destroy us?"*

It took me a long time to believe God's answer. No. He did not bring us into the desert to destroy us. Instead, he led me into the desert to humble me, to test me, and to know what was in my heart. Just as he will surely do to you at one time or another on your journey. Perhaps you're facing such a time right now.

When God speaks of humbling us, he doesn't mean beating us down or humiliating us. Instead, he means to bless us with a *right conception* of who we are so that we are prepared to be *exalted* by him. When God exalts us, no one can tear us down. When God exalts us, there can be no room for pride.

> Humble yourselves in the sight of the Lord, and He will exalt you. And of what does the exaltation consist? The highest glory of man is in being only a vessel, to receive and enjoy and show forth the glory of God. It can do this only as it is willing to be nothing in itself so that God may be all. Water always fills the lowest places first. The lower, the emptier man lies before God, the speedier and the fuller the inflow of the divine glory will be.[2]

[2]Andrew Murray, *Humility* (Springdale, Pa.: Whitaker House, 1982). More recently, Bethany House Publishers released a complete library of Andrew Murray's writings. Check it out!

Why is it so important for God to humble us, to test us, to know what's in our hearts? Because God knows that after the desert of testing comes the Promised Land. This brings us to the final two questions: *What potential pitfalls does God warn them against?* and *What relevance does the Deuteronomy 8 passage—"entering into the Promised Land"—have for your life?* Let's review the relevant portion.

> When you have eaten and are satisfied, praise the Lord your God for the good land he has given you. Be careful that you do not forget the Lord your God, failing to observe his commands, his laws and his decrees that I am giving you this day. Otherwise, when you eat and are satisfied, when you build fine houses and settle down, and when your herds and flocks grow large and your silver and gold increase and all you have is multiplied, then your heart will become proud and you will forget the Lord your God, who brought you out of Egypt, out of the land of slavery. (vv. 10–14)

The greatest pitfall of the Promised Land is pride. Ultimately pride leads to unbelief. Pride says, "I don't need God." Unbelief takes pride a step further and concludes, "God doesn't even exist." It's the old "I'm a self-made man and I worship my Creator" routine.

God wants better for us. He wants us to continue to rely on him for our daily bread, even when we can afford a brand-new breadmaker. If your heart is humble before God, you'll never forget that every good thing is directly from his hand and that awareness is a greater blessing than anything the Promised Land has to offer.

Reflections Along the Journey

1. Why does God allow us to endure a desert of testing?

2. Are you in the midst of a desert right now? Describe. If not, recall a desert experience and the lessons you learned from it.

3. Write out a prayer asking God to give you a heart of humility.

4. What key lesson did you glean from today's study?

Freedom Truths:

- The greatest potential pitfall of the Promised Land is pride.
- When you enter the Promised Land, never forget who brought you there.

Day Five

Free to Embrace Both the Price and the Privilege

I can't even begin to describe to you the spiritual and emotional battles I've endured while writing this book. They are beyond my comprehension, beyond my ability to articulate. I guess it's just the price I pay for the privilege I enjoy of being used by God in this way. I remember another time—my speaking ministry was just beginning to take off—when I went through intense spiritual warfare. I remember crying out to God, *"Deliver me. NOW."* Since he was taking too long, I tried various ways to deliver myself. How do you think that worked out?

Right.

Anyway, after all my attempts to deliver myself had failed, I decided to take a walk so I could have a good cry and get serious about feeling sorry for myself. I don't know about you, but when I try to deliver myself, I invariably make a fool of myself and I usually tick a few people off in the process. So I sat down on a rock and began complaining to God. I mean, if he hadn't taken so long to deliver me, I wouldn't have tried to deliver myself. I wouldn't have made a fool of myself, no one would be mad at me, and none of this stuff would have happened. See, it was all God's fault!

Finally, I told God I had had enough: "That's it. Just take this from me; this gift-curse you've given me. Let me be NORMAL." I told him all about the woman who had the life I wanted. "Why can't my life be like hers? Why can't I BE like her?" This was one of those rare moments when God decided to respond to one of my tantrums in a powerful, unmistakable way. So he spoke to me with a clarity I've enjoyed on only a few prior occasions:

"Would you really trade places with her?" he asked. *"Would you really give up all the miracles I've worked in your life? Would you really give up the joy of being used by me? If that's what you want, I will take*

my gift from you. But you can't have it both ways. You can't be my servant and lead a normal life. THE PRIVILEGE COMES AT A PRICE. I've given you the privilege, but you must be willing to pay the price. Now, what is it going to be?"

I wept. I knew he meant business. I agreed to pay the price secretly hoping that since I was being so agreeable he'd *lower* it. He hasn't lowered it; if anything, he has raised it.

I thank God for the privilege he has given me to share this journey with you. I hope it has made a difference in your life. If it has, I would love to hear from you. You'll find my home address and e-mail address with my bio at the front of this book. I know in my heart that if my message can change just one life, it was well worth the price.

We do indeed have a God who is able to deliver us. We have a God who can set us free. So enter in, my friend. Begin to live in absolute freedom.

Reflections Along the Journey

1. Take this opportunity to recall some of the most significant lessons you've learned on your ten-week journey to living in absolute freedom.

2. Write out a prayer to God, thanking him for the work he has done in setting you free.

3. What key lesson did you glean from today's study?

4. Write out this week's verse from memory.

Freedom Truths:

- We have a God who is able to deliver us.
- Please write to Donna and share with her how God has set you free through this study.

Weekly Review

See if you can fill in the seven steps toward living in absolute freedom. You should know them by now! But look in the back of the book if you need help.

F _____ your bondage

R _____ your Deliverer

E _____ your liberty

E _____ your fellow slaves

D _____ yourself in God

O _____ pockets of resistance

M _____ forward in absolute freedom

Steps to Freedom

1. *Know that God loves you.* "For God so loved the world that he gave his one and only son, that whoever believes in him shall not perish but have eternal life" (John 3:16).
2. *Acknowledge your sin.* "For all have sinned and fall short of the glory of God" (Romans 3:23).
3. *Turn from sin.* "Therefore do not let sin reign in your mortal body so that you obey its evil desires. Do not offer the parts of your body to sin, as instruments of wickedness, but rather offer yourselves to God" (Romans 6:12–13).
4. *Accept that Jesus is the only way.* "I am the way and the truth and the life. No one comes to the father except through me" (John 14:6). "Salvation is found in no one else, for there is no other name under heaven given to men by which we must be saved" (Acts 4:12).
5. *Realize that Jesus paid the penalty for your sins.* "But he was pierced for our transgressions, he was crushed for our iniquities; the punishment that brought us peace was upon him, and by his wounds we are healed. We all, like sheep, have gone astray, each of us has turned to his own way; and the Lord has laid on him the iniquity of us all" (Isaiah 53:5–6).
6. *Receive Jesus as your Savior.* "Here I am! I stand at the door and knock. If anyone hears my voice and opens the door, I will go in and eat with him, and he with me" (Revelation 3:20). "Yet to all who received him, to those who believed in his name, he gave the right to become children of God" (John 1:12).

A Note to Leaders

Dear Bible Study Leaders:

I want to thank you for choosing *Living in Absolute Freedom*, not just for your own use, but to share with the women God has entrusted to your care. It's a great honor to know that among all the excellent Bible study materials available, you consider my book worthwhile.

I pray that this journey will lead you into a deeper love relationship with God and into closer fellowship with the women who participate.

When I wrote *Becoming a Vessel God Can Use*, I urged readers to take the study one day at a time, to resist the temptation to rush through. I have since heard how to read my books from many people that I don't even know. The best way, so I'm told, is to quickly read through the entire book without looking at the questions. You might instruct the women in your group to set aside a day or a long weekend to tackle the project. Then, once they have the overview, they can work through the book one day at a time.

Another piece of feedback I'd like to pass along is this: Whenever possible, use a visual. There's so much imagery associated with slavery throughout the book, so bring it to life in a concrete way. In particular, I would urge you to make use of the ceremony described in Week 7, Day 5.

Bring the study to life, and it will bring life to the lives of those who participate. Speaking of participants, I'm including a Participant Profile worksheet. Please make photocopies of it to use with your class. During your first meeting, ask each person to complete the questionnaire. Allow plenty of time for this exercise. The insight you will gain will be extremely valuable as you seek to meet the needs of each woman. Once everyone has finished, spend time discussing their responses, *but don't call on anyone*. People do not like to be put on the spot, so let them know from the beginning that your policy is to encourage—but not require—participation in the discussion.

Make it a point to contact each woman on a regular basis *outside* the classroom environment. It could be a phone call, a note card, or a trip to the park together. The key is to demonstrate a personal interest in their spiritual growth and well-being. The Profile worksheets will give you a good place to start in understanding each woman's needs and in initiating conversation.

The one exception to the "not putting people on the spot" rule is the Memory Verse Cards, which you'll find at the back of the book. Each week, at the very beginning of class, ask each woman to recite her verse from memory. Do it in a spirit of fun and out of a desire to "spur one another on toward love and good deeds." Be sensitive, and avoid embarrassing anyone. Nevertheless, when the women come to understand that they will be expected to recite their verse, almost all will rise to the occasion and put in the extra effort required.

If women will carry their memory verse cards with them wherever they go, there is absolutely no reason why they can't memorize one verse per week. You may find it helpful to review the tips provided in my previous book, *Walking in Total God-Confidence* (Week 6, Day 4, "Knowing God's Word by Heart"). Using these techniques, anyone can learn to memorize Scripture effectively.

Along with each week's memory verse, I have also included a few key thoughts to summarize the lesson. These do not have to be memorized but will help the women get the most out of the study.

Finally, you'll notice that there is a Weekly Review Test included each week. It's always the same test, but hopefully the women will get better and better scores. Again, make it a point to take the test as a group every week by reciting in unison the seven steps on the journey to Living in Absolute Freedom.

When your group successfully completes the study, I would love nothing more than to receive a photograph of all you beautiful women. I like to put these on the wall of my home office to prevent me from "growing weary in well-doing." I really cherish every letter I receive, although I must admit I'm not that great about writing back. Just know in advance, you'll do the heart of this Princess some good!

His vessel,
Donna Partow
P.O. Box 842
Payson, AZ 85541
donnapartow@cybertrails.com

Participant Profile Sheet

Name: _____ Phone: _____

Address: _____

_____

_____

Reason for enrolling in this class: _____

_____

_____

_____

_____

What is the most pressing problem/challenge in your life right now?

_____

_____

_____

How can this class (and your fellow classmates) help you cope more effectively?

_____

_____

_____

_____

How do you want your life to be different at the end of this study?

_____

_____

_____

_____

What are some specific habits you want to improve?

_____

_____

_____

_____

_____

List five things you expect from a women's Bible study. (Indicate things you like/dislike.)

1. _____

2. _____

3. _____

4. _____

5. _____

Thinking back on prior experiences with Bible studies, what motivated you to finish a class? What might cause you to drop out of a class?

_____

_____

_____

_____

How can your leader help you to get the most out of this class?

_____

_____

_____

_____

_____

Steps to Freedom

- FACE your bondage
- RECEIVE your Deliverer
- EMBRACE your liberty
- EMANCIPATE your fellow slaves
- DELIGHT yourself in God
- OVERCOME pockets of resistance
- MOVE forward in absolute freedom

Become a Woman of True Confidence

A 10-week journey that will change your life!

A TEN-WEEK JOURNEY TO

WALKING IN TOTAL

God-Confidence

DONNA PARTOW

AUTHOR OF THE BESTSELLER
Becoming a Vessel God Can Use

Women all around the world have discovered the life-changing power of *Becoming a Vessel God Can Use*. Now bestselling author Donna Partow delivers a remarkable new book.

Walking in Total God-Confidence helps women discover real confidence: the unshakable assurance that comes not from self-reliance, but from "God-confidence." God-confidence is the absolute belief that God can do anything and everything He wants to do through you—regardless of your upbringing, circumstances, past successes or failures. This exciting ten-week journey will inspire you to rely completely on God for your confidence and sense of value and worth.

Ideal for group Bible studies or individual use!

Thank you for selecting a book from
BETHANY HOUSE PUBLISHERS

Bethany House Publishers is a ministry of Bethany Fellowship International, an interdenominational, nonprofit organization committed to spreading the Good News of Jesus Christ around the world through evangelism, church planting, literature distribution, and care for those in need. Missionary training is offered through Bethany College of Missions.

Bethany Fellowship International is a member of the National Association of Evangelicals and subscribes to its statement of faith. If you would like further information, please contact:

Bethany Fellowship International
6820 Auto Club Road
Minneapolis, MN 55438 USA